FROM ST. AUGUSTINE
TO WILLIAM TEMPLE

FROM ST. AUGUSTINE TO WILLIAM TEMPLE

Eight Studies in Christian Leadership

By

VIVIAN H. H. GREEN, M.A., B.D.

Biography Index Reprint Series

 BOOKS FOR LIBRARIES PRESS
FREEPORT, NEW YORK

First Published 1948

Reprinted 1971 by arrangement with Dr. V. H. H. Green

INTERNATIONAL STANDARD BOOK NUMBER:
0-8369-8060-3

LIBRARY OF CONGRESS CATALOG CARD NUMBER:
72-148213

PRINTED IN THE UNITED STATES OF AMERICA

Preface

THIS BOOK consists of eight essays on representative figures in the history of the Christian Church, about whose significance the ordinary reader is often curiously ill-informed. Moreover, the character of each man's message was powerfully affected by the nature of the personal or world-crisis, through which he lived, in most cases by both. Such a crisis formed an essential factor in creating a message or mission which became the intellectual and spiritual response to the challenge of the age.

The relevance of these brief essays to our own times may not be neglected. As I write, I am more convinced than ever that mankind is faced, far more urgently than it was a century ago, by the alternative of disruptive chaos, which would precede the new Dark Ages, or constructive Christian civilization. And it is depressingly obvious that there is no one nor yet a group of men whose spiritual vitality or intellectual genius can lead even one nation or continent, let alone the world, out of the contemporary "Slough of Despond". But it is a lesson of history that past crises have sometimes generated the constructive leader, in the spiritual sense of the phrase, who has given a fresh and invigorating call to society. Whether the Church—and the Church of England in particular—bereft of William Temple, may be able to do so in the future, history alone will record, but hapless and helpless millions, often deceived and exploited by self-interested cliques and rulers, await the real call to the spiritual change which, fundamentally, must precede all realistic political and social transformation.

The book makes no pretensions to original research, but I hope that it may interest and even instruct its readers. There is a short bibliography at the close of each essay which gives a list of the books to which I am more particularly indebted.

VIVIAN H. H. GREEN.

Sherborne,
March 17th, 1948.

Contents

I. St. Augustine of Hippo

" IT WAS on the fifteenth of October in the gloom of evening, as I sat musing on the Capitol, while the barefooted friars were chanting their litanies in the temple of Jupiter, that I conceived the first thought of my history. My original plan was confined to the decay of the City; my reading and reflection pointed to that aim; but several years elapsed . . . before I grappled with the decline and fall of the Roman Empire.'' It was in this way that the dapper, complacent and strikingly erudite Mr. Edward Gibbon was inspired to write the most thrilling of all histories, the story of the collapse of the great Mediterranean Empire which was for so long focused on the city of Rome. In splendid, rhymthic prose, decorous and firm, the story proceeds through fourteen centuries to its appointed close, the death of the last of the Roman Emperors in the breach which the invading Turks had made in the walls of Constantinople. Yet this most gifted of historians had one defect. He lacked the power to dwell in the period of history which he sought to record. He can tell us what Eusebius advised or what Zosimus chronicled, but he is supremely unmoved by the emotions which fraught religious controversy, or by the intensity of passion and the apathy of culture which accompanied the empire's closing years. To some extent, indeed, unaware of the impending crisis which confronted his own contemporary world, spending the last years of his life in tranquil seclusion with Deyverdun by the placid waters of the Lake of Geneva,

9

Mr. Gibbon was unable to vitalize the tremendous issues which he had described with so fine a felicity of style and learning.

This Roman world which bordered the Mediterranean lake and stretched far inland to the *limes* of the Rhine and the Danube, whose legions marched along the wall which Hadrian had built under the cold northern skies of Britain or on the fierce sands of Mesopotamia, seemed the inevitable foundation of world civilization. If it owed much in beauty and in thought to the Greeks whom it had brought under its rule, and something more in commercial acumen to the peoples of the east, its own efficient administration was stamped with genius. The long, straight roads carried a continuous stream of traffic from one corner of the empire to the other, whilst imperial supervision gave freedom from piracy and theft on land and sea. The buildings and temples of an essentially urban civilization were imposing, more than anything else conveying to the conquered who were brought through the busy streets of the capital, its power and eternity. Aqueducts supplied its cities with water; its houses were well drained and warmed;[1] but the empire's accomplishments were not wholly material. The magnificent structure of law, which formed the foundation of modern, common and international law, was fashioned by the Ulpians and Trebonians whose stability of demeanour contrasted so strikingly with the shoddy elegance of later emperors. The vast empire was ruled by an efficient and relatively honest civil service which upheld the dignity and prestige of the emperor, even if the standards of justice varied from province to province and from age to age. Furthermore, this civilization was universal. Spaniards and Thracians presided over the majesty of an empire whose

---

[1] On life in the capital of the Empire, consult J. Carcopino, *Daily life in Ancient Rome*. (Trs. H. T. Rowell, 1941.)

tongue was one, whose loyalty was focused on the personality of a man who surrounded himself with an increasing degree of autocratic pomp. The imperfections of Roman imperialism were many and varied; the social structure of the empire was as profoundly unjust as the society itself was morally inadequate. The austere dignity of the early senator compared favourably with the sycophantic and sybaritic Roman of the later days. There was at all times a turbulent city mob waiting to be fed with doles of bread and unpleasantly sadistic entertainments in the magnificent amphitheatres, while a rural proletariat tilled the vineyards and fields of the wealthy aristocracy. And yet such a society seemed infinite, even amidst the economic crisis of the third century. It was unthinkable that a day should come when Rome would stand as Jerusalem had stood, a city without an empire, inhabited by the barbarian tribes which raided the frontier outposts hundreds of miles away.

It was this Roman Empire which chambered the young Christian Church. If there was an underlying dichotomy which made the Christian place his loyalty to God before the emperor and prefer the eagerly awaited coming of Christ to the favour of the court, there could be no question about the close relationship existing between the two institutions, even in the days of misunderstanding and sporadic persecution which marked their early history. Everything conspired to bring this about; St. Paul himself would not disown Roman citizenship with its privileges and prestige-value. Roman law and custom formed the environment in which the oriental religion and Hellenic philosophy worked together under the impetus of the Incarnation of Jesus Christ to form the Church of God. Just as the dioceses of the Church were modelled on the organization of the Roman Empire, so the bishop of its capital city became, in some sense, the spiritual counterpart of imperial and secular majesty, the final court of appeal, the centre of jurisdiction, the proclaimer of accepted doctrine. If Greek still continued to be the more normal means of expression for worship and communication, Latin soon became of equal importance, a cherished possession of the Christian community both in daily life and in the offering of worship which the Catholic Church has never wholly abandoned. The procedure of councils, like the law which they formulated, was modelled on and influenced by what the ordinary citizen knew about the activities of secular courts and conferences. Finally, the emperor had become a Christian. The second of the able reforming emperors of the fourth century, Constantine the Great, had seen that a vigorous and loyal minority was an asset which he could not overlook in his struggle for mastery. His friend and adviser, Bishop Eusebius, as well as the pagan historian, Nazarius, tell how the emperor saw a vision in the sky on the eve of a critical battle, a banner bearing the symbolic "In Hoc Signo, Vince". Scholars have differed greatly about the sincerity of the imperial conversion which, in more ways than one, certainly left much to be desired. But whether the emperor was influenced by politics or some vague comprehension of a new syncretistic religion which combined the powers of the pagan deities with a more vital and imposing faith, matters little besides the great fact that the empire had become officially Christian. Paganism became an underground movement, slowly losing its hold over the intellectual classes, retaining a superstitious grip over the peasants and reappearing in troubled and fanciful forms to the discomfort of the Church in later times, but nevertheless depressed and unimportant. The Church stood imposing, divided by different groups which disputed as to the meaning of the Incarnation of Christ, yet powerful and influential, increasingly rich and decisive in its claims.

"Thou hast conquered, O Galilean", Theodoret makes the Emperor Julian say after he saw that death on a Persian battlefield had brought the last attempt to reimpose paganism on the empire to failure; but there were signs, as some of the more prescient Christians noted, that the Church of Bishop Damasus of Rome had moved far away from the community in the upper room at Jerusalem.

The pressure of time on history reveals that change and decay form an essential ingredient in the life of all civilized societies. Sixteen civilizations had already perished without leaving behind a single sign of vitality that could ensure their continuity. By the middle of the fourth century the mirror of Roman society was slowly cracking. Whether it would be resolved into a thousand shivering fragments or whether it would undergo in the heat of conflict a metamorphosis which would enable it to continue in a changed shape, seemed uncertain. It was clear that the reforms which the emperors, Diocletian and Constantine, had initiated in the administration and economic system of the empire had not stemmed the march towards a further crisis, for what had been originally intended as a temporary measure had become permanent and static. There were, everywhere, signs of growing disorder which rivalry for the imperial throne only served to stimulate. The roads and the seas became afflicted by robbers, while the burden of provincial and imperial taxes rose to oppressive heights. The municipal officials, the *curiales,* with whom the responsibility for raising the revenue lay, tried in vain to evade the obligations which were placed upon them. They, like everyone else, were obliged to keep to the profession which their fathers had held before them. The thread of discontent became more perceptible in the crowded slums of the great cities and amidst the rural proletariat that worked the great *latifundia* or landed estates. It became an increasingly familiar sight to see barbarian soldiers in the streets and roads, hard men, strong fighters, awe-inspired by the might of Rome but regardless of her supine citizens. For men preferred to mutilate themselves rather than serve away from home on the far and dangerous imperial frontiers. But was danger so far away? A shiver of incredible horror ran through Christian and pagan alike in 410, when Alaric the Goth occupied the capital city of the empire. In far away Bethlehem the Christian ascetic, Jerome, momentarily forgot his controversies and studies in the stifling reality of a frightening moment of history: "My voice left me and sobs choked my speech. The city which had conquered the whole world is herself captive. . . . For long I remained silent, bethinking me well that this was a time for weeping." The moment passed, leaving the marbles of the imperial palaces and the tenemented slums of Ostia much as they had been before, but the experience was vital. The atmosphere of the age portended change which no man could resist. In the last century and a half of the western empire there was a curious feeling of boredom and indifference, through which ripples of culture and laughter floated on the soft and sultry evening air. Of what does the great senator, Quintus Aurelius Symmachus, write in these critical days of barbarian invasion? He wants to know how the Saxon gladiators, who had, perhaps justifiably, gone on strike, had strangled themselves, and if the crocodiles had arrived, or how glad he is that it is his friend's birthday. Life maintained its even flow: the theatres were filled; the shows went on and the corn was gathered in on the rural estates; polite conversation flourished. The Roman Empire seemed the natural corollary of existence. There was some truth in the satirical Salvianus' remark that the "Roman Empire was laughing when it died".

But there was, in fact, a deep and underlying crisis which the sterility of contemporary literature and its aimless concern with rhetoric and similar studies reveals. The western empire was in process of slow disintegration, or, perhaps, metamorphosis would be a better word since the barbarians who wrought the ruin constituted themselves the heirs of the dying tradition. The old imperial order was breaking up, spreading economic, social and administrative chaos as it went. The Romans who saw something of what was happening were so greatly perplexed at the turn of events that many asserted, as they had done in Cyprian's time a century earlier, that the gods who had protected the fortunes of Rome had taken umbrage at their treatment. It was the Christians who had ruined the empire, for it was they who had slain its ancient traditions and instituted a new order in life and society with which the gods disagreed. Even the Roman Christian found the problem mind-reeling. The transitional period inevitably called forth a struggle of great mental intensity in the minds of all thoughtful men. What was the Christian's attitude to the crisis of his time, and to what order in society could he look for security and hope? Standing in the twilight of a great age, he could not discern the nature of the future. If the parent society which was indissolubly associated with his life vanished, what was to take its place, and if he were a Christian, what of the Church which that society had shielded?

It is in this context that Augustine's life takes on significance and meaning, for no man so well understood the nature of the spiritual crisis of his time or was so well prepared to meet it. His early life formed in some ways an analogical preparation for his later task, since it was, as he himself tells us in his *Confessions*, a conflict between the true order in life and nature to which his real self was attracted, and the undisciplined luxury of selfish aims which proved the easier road. The struggle was intense, prolonged and left so indelible a stamp on Augustine's personality that if it brought him to the throne of divine love, its burning ardour at times strained human tolerance. He was born on November 13th, 354, at Tagaste, a small town in the Roman province of Numidia where his father, Patricius, was an official. Viewing his easy-going[1] pagan father, ambitious in worldly matters for his son, through the somewhat glazed eyes of later age, he suggests that there were differences of temperament that made filial love difficult. Patricius died when Augustine was seventeen. On the other hand, the relations between Augustine and his mother, Monica, a devout Christian woman of high principle and sterling personality, were extremely close. Even when Augustine defied his mother, he was obliged to resort to subterfuge to avoid the heart-shaking realization of her displeasure. If his later account is to be trusted, his schooldays were improvident, rash, sensuous; "out of the muddy concupiscence of the flesh and the bubblings of youth, mists fumed up which beclouded and overcast my heart, that I could not discern the clear brightness of love, from the fog of lustfulness. Both did confusedly boil in me, and hurried my unstayed youth over the precipice of unholy desires, and sunk me in a gulf of flagitiousness." If such experiences are the commonplaces of religious and other men, on the brink of adolescence, they need not be gain-said. His account of a raid on a pear orchard contains the quintessence of youthful yet not very blameworthy irrespon-sibility: "A pear tree there was near our vineyard, laden with fruit, tempting neither for colour nor taste. To shake and rob this, some lewd young fellows of us went, late one night (having according to our pestilent custom prolonged our sports in the streets till then) and took huge loads, not

---

[1] Tho "Sicut benevolentia praecipuus ita ira fervidus."

for our eating, but to fling to the very hogs, having only
tasted them.'' These things do not reveal, as the conscious
stricken autobiographer afterwards felt, the inner reality of
ancient sin, and yet they suggest, what later events confirmed, that there was little stability and some want of
purpose in the young man. There was a natural eagerness
for learning what he liked, for Latin rather than Greek, a
discerning aptitude and ability but as yet little that could
be the father of the man.

The unsatisfied pilgrimage continued for well-nigh
twenty years. At the University of Carthage his life drifted
between inner restlessness and dissipation. "Here," he
told his listeners at a much later date, "in this very city I
led an evil life, I confess it. And just as I rejoice over
God's grace in me, so for my evil past I what? Shall I say
'grieve'? Certainly I would were I now as I then was.
Shall I say 'rejoice'? No, for that I cannot say, for would
that I had never been such! For I suffer torture in my
thoughts; I have to struggle against evil suggestions; my
conflict with the enemy who tempts me is a daily one,
well-nigh an unceasing one." Beneath the native indisci-
pline of mind and body which directed so many of his
activities in the heated atmosphere of this busy university
city, there was an underlying gravity of mind which made
him acutely aware of his dissatisfaction and eager to find a
solution to the problems of life. It was this which drew
him to Manichaeism, a creed popular in contemporary
Carthage. Its founder, a Persian ascetic called Mani who
lived in the third century, had concluded that the universe
had one essential theme, the constant struggle between
good and evil. In the great primal battle, evil had warred
against good with such effect that God's chosen champion,
His Son, had been himself led into captivity. But the light
particles remained alive in the surrounding darkness, only

awaiting their opportunity to secure freedom. Man's personality embodies the continuous conflict, but, stimulated by the teaching of the prophets amongst whom Jesus was included, man has the power to free himself gradually from the domination of evil. What could be a more attractive or rational creed to a young man beset by desire but seriously concerned with the pursuit of perfection?[1] To the grief of his mother, Monica, Augustine became a Manichaean; he found consolation for his desires by taking a mistress and for his spiritual intentions through the study of philosophy. Cicero's *Hortensius* "altered my affections and turned my prayers to Thyself, O Lord", but the "immortality of wisdom" for which his soul ached was as yet denied him. He was, perhaps, not as unhappy as his later references to this period of his life might suggest, but he was inwardly troubled, both by the inadequacy of his vocation and his failure to achieve intellectual and spiritual calm. After finishing his course of studies at the University, he taught rhetoric, a subject which in itself reflects the barren nature of contemporary scholarship. It may be supposed that his lack of interest in his own subject would account for the difficulties he sustained in keeping order among his unruly students. After a short visit to Rome, he was offered a professorship at Milan in 384. But it was hardly possible that the change of atmosphere would bring him peace. Convinced that the Manichaeans had over-emphasized the material nature of reality, he concluded that he ought to leave their sect; yet this would still leave him without a faith, an agnostic who could not yet approach or comprehend spiritual reality. Meanwhile, he found some consolation in the teaching of the Neoplatonists, the third-century philosophers who discerned in the writings of the

[1] On its interesting later medieval proliferations, consult J. C. S. Runciman, *The Medieval Manichee*, 1947.

great Greek philosopher, spiritual truths approaching Christianity.

Nevertheless, the place and the date of Augustine's departure to Italy were both of tremendous significance.

Damasus, the Pope of Rome who died in 384, had brought the papal power to a greater height than any of his predecessors. He was a vigorous personality whose election to the pontificate had been accompanied by rioting in which no less than 137 people had been killed.[1] That this could happen openly in the streets of Rome was a tribute to the secular security of the Church, but it was equally well a manifestation of a malaise which Damasus' pontificate, for all its success, did very little to alleviate. Constantine's acceptance of Christianity as the official religion of the state at the beginning of the fourth century, had been followed by the absorbtion of vast numbers of nominal Christians into the Church. This had resulted in a secularization of the Christian life which divisions within the Church had only encouraged further. The standards of Christian life, as well as the nature of Christian teaching, all suffered from the increasingly mundane character of the Church. Every challenge, however, evokes a response. If the pontificate of Damasus saw a movement in this direction, it also witnessed the departure of his secretary, Jerome, to an ascetic existence in Palestine and the resurgence of the monastic movement, which had originated as a protest against the lowering of standards. No one played so pre-eminent a part in this response as the bishop of the important Italian city of Milan, Ambrose. The episcopate which had been practically forced upon the unwilling prefect revealed his great gifts as an administrator and his care and love for his flock. Turbulent as were the Milanese, they realized that they had a decisive leader and

[1] Consult T. G. Jalland, *The Church and the Papacy*, 1944, 238 f.

a man of noble character in their bishop. Augustine's arrival in Milan had therefore far more than purely personal significance. Although he was not yet a Christian, had never been baptized, his spiritual and mental struggle was representative of the inner crisis which was dividing the Church and the Roman world. And Ambrose was to be the one man who could apply the challenge of the gospel to the professor of rhetoric and secure a response. The sermons of the bishop produced a profound effect, for if he had been originally drawn by Ambrose's learning and eloquence, he stayed to learn wisdom. "So it was that I came to Milan and to Ambrose the bishop, known to the whole world as among the best of men, Thy devout servant; whose eloquent discourse did then plentifully dispense unto Thy people the flour of Thy wheat, the gladness of Thy oil, and the sober inebriation of Thy wine. To him was I unknowingly led by Thee, that by him I might knowingly be led to Thee." Yet it was not as easy as all that. Augustine was not a man who would willingly renounce his former beliefs and accept a new faith until he had been convinced intellectually. If he began to attend church regularly, he was unwilling to throw off his mistress or surrender his past reputation. "Give me chastity and continence, only not yet." On the steps of the garden he fought out the battle. "I was troubled in spirit, most vehemently indignant that I entered not into Thy will and covenant, O my God, which all my bones cried out unto me to enter, and praised it to the skies." His friend, Alypius, was with him, but he could not help, for the struggle had reached a climax where the decision would only be fought out with God by Augustine himself. "I cast myself down I know not how, under a certain fig-tree, giving full vent to my tears; and the floods of mine eyes gushed out, an acceptable sacrifice to Thee. And, not indeed in these words, to yet this purpose, spake I much unto Thee; And Thou, O Lord, how long? . . . I sent up these sorrowful words; How long —how long, 'tomorrow and tomorrow?' Why not now? Why not is there this hour an end to my uncleanness? So sat I speaking, and weeping in the most bitter contrition of my heart, when lo! I heard from a neighbouring house a voice, as of a boy or girl, I know not, chanting, and oft repeating, 'Take up and read; take up and read'. Instantly, my countenance altered, I began to think most intently, whether children were wont in any kind of play to sing such words; nor could I remember ever to have heard the like. So, checking the torrent of my tears, I arose; interpreting it to be no other than a command from God to open the book and to read the first chapter I should find. . . . Eagerly then I returned to the place where Alypius was sitting; for there had I laid the volume of the Apostle, when I arose thence. I seized, opened and in silence read that section on which my eyes first fell; Not in rioting and drunkenness, not in chambering and wantonness, not in strife and envying; but put ye on the Lord Jesus Christ, and make not provision for the flesh, in concupiscence. No further would I read, nor needed I; for instantly at the end of this sentence, by a light as it were of serenity infused into my heart, all the darkness of doubt vanished away." "Tolle et lege", were words of the most critical significance, for they had affected what years of wandering in mind and spirit had been unable to bring out. So long in the desert places of the mind was followed by an entry into green pastures. Augustine resigned his professorship and with his mother and a group of disciples, retired into the country to Cassiciacum to prepare for baptism. There was quietness and serenity about these autumn and early winter days in the country villa; he paints a charming impression of the discussions which he had with his friends under the shade of the tree in the sunny fields. Through the open window of his room he could hear the murmur of the little brook, the symbol of an infinity which gave repose and certainty to his own ordered thoughts. The baptism ceremony took place at Easter, 387; "we were baptized and all the anxiety about past life slipped away from us. In those days I could never be sated with the indescribable sweetness that overwhelmed me when I recalled the profundity of Thy counsels wherewith Thou didst secure the salvation of the human race. How I wept when I listened with deep emotion to the hymns and canticles so sweetly sung in Thy Church; as the sound of them rang in my ears truth shone so clearly in my heart and the devoutest feelings so flooded my soul that tears ran down my cheeks and all was well with me."

And yet even if the mind was now at rest, the way was still steep and narrow. It seemed as if Augustine had found faith only that he might be the more strengthened to withstand the trials that were to confront him. He had already sent his mistress back to North Africa. Some have criticized his action as unfeeling but the loyalty and the friendship which undoubtedly characterized their relationship did not constitute love, nor could the new-found love which Augustine had experienced, have condoned so irregular a relationship. The breach must, nevertheless, have constituted an emotional challenge. His mother's death was far more of a blow, even if she died knowing that her most cherished ambition had been attained. By the window at Ostia, whither he had gone from Rome, they had a final conversation touched and adorned by Monica's steadfast faith; "nothing is far from God; no reason to fear He will find it difficult at the end of the world to know whence to raise me." Augustine's son, Adeodatus, who had been greatly attached to his grandmother, died soon after. Bereft of his mother, changed in faith, he returned to Africa to his native town of Tagaste.

The long period of strain was followed by one of consolidation. The literature and rhetoric to which he had once devoted so great a portion of his time were put away. Philosophy and theology formed the staple food of the mind between 388 and 391. Ever unwearying, he brought all his massive intellect and heightened spirituality to bear on problems of eternal moment; it was now that he wrote his famous treatises on the Immortality of the Soul, on Music, on the Extensity of the Soul and on Free Will. His life was simple and austere. Henceforth, he would devote himself to divine learning. Even if he failed to realize it, this was to some extent an abdication of his mission. His powers of criticism were acute, his ability to analyse and synthesize were above the ordinary while his past experience had enriched his mind and gave vitality to his discussions. Yet the crisis of the Roman world was not of a specifically intellectual or philosophical nature. It was simply that disorder was rife, that the barbarians were tumbling over the frontiers, that the empire of the west was controlled by an effete pietist named Honorius, that economic and social chaos threatened the future of an institution which seemed inseparable from civilization. A man who would give himself up solely to the study of infinite problems might be said to be betraying his responsibility to the finite world.

As it happened, circumstances took the decision out of Augustine's hands. Unexpectedly ordained priest in 391-2, he was consecrated co-adjutor bishop to Valerius, the infirm Bishop of Hippo, four years later. He had no wish to undertake so responsible a position, for he was now forty-one years of age, only recently relieved from prolonged mental tension. He would have much preferred to have lived a secluded and ascetic life as a scholar, but it was clear that if he had confronted and triumphed in his own personal crisis, he had not yet thoroughly faced the much greater challenge of his age. If it is given to some men to live away from the realities of a world situation, it is given to very few men to become either an Athanasius or an Augustine. Reluctant as he was to assume responsibility, he found that the turbulent Romans of Africa were too much for him. "So much did I dread being made a Bishop that when I found that God's servants were talking seriously about the reputation I had made I was careful not to go to places where I knew there was no Bishop. . . . But I came to this city to see a friend whom I thought I could win over to God's service and who might perhaps enter our monastery. I felt quite safe since a Bishop was in occupation of the see. But I was caught and made a priest and once that step had been taken I was made a Bishop." His diocesan city, Hippo, was fronted by the Mediterranean and backed by a plain full of terraced vineyards and olive groves and cooled by the river Sebus. The North African population over whose spiritual destinies Augustine now presided, had a long tradition of political and ecclesiastical turbulence, which even the vital will of their new bishop could not, as in the case of Melania and Pinian, completely overrule. The heresies which disturbed the Church's life had always found fertile soil amidst the discontented proletariat of Rome's African provinces. Augustine was, in fact, faced by a task much greater than the personal crisis which he had recently met. He recognized that his people came before his studies, so that "my ecclesiastical preoccupations wholly preclude me from devoting myself to any other study than such as is necessary for the instruction of my flock".

The more he spent himself, the more he found to do.

As he became older, he suffered from the change of climate, while insomnia reduced his energy. Yet the strain of the world crisis rather than ill-health, sapped his resources. At the same time, it also drew from him his most significant contribution to the Christian philosophy of existence. The situation in the depopulated and exhausted empire was deteriorating steadily. The emperor's barbarian general, the Vandal Stilicho, spent his time in crushing revolts conjured up by tribal ambition and imperial divisions. In 401 the Visigothic leader, Alaric, swept down into Italy from Illyricum to receive a check from Stilicho's troops at Pollentia. But able as Stilicho was, he could not stem the tide which flowed over every frontier and flooded through the land. The Vandals, Alans and Goths, under Radagaisus, renewed their rebellion. Other tribes crossed the Rhine and ravaged Gaul throughout 407. Rebel commanders renounced their loyalty to the empire. Stilicho, who had warded off these attacks with consummate skill, fell a victim to treachery at home. His successor, the eunuch Olympius, was incapable and incompetent. While the emperor remained in comfortable confinement behind the well-fortified outposts of Ravenna, the Goths entered Italy under Alaric, held the capital city twice to ransom and on the third occasion stormed and sacked it. The revulsion was tremendous. The city which symbolized the imperialism of Rome, its outstanding civilization, law and order, had fallen to a wandering barbarian tribe. The western empire survived for another sixty-six years, for Alaric died just as he was about to cross over into Africa. But Rome was symbolically transmuted and changed when he entered it.

To Augustine in distant Africa the fall of Rome constituted the supreme challenge. Within the coming years the situation in North Africa was to worsen, for the last years of his episcopate witnessed the complete disintegration of imperial unity. In Africa, Count Boniface invited the Vandals to come to his support, only to find that the saviours whose aid he had sought were to prove his ruin. The remains of Count Boniface's legions were besieged in Hippo as the old and tired bishop lay ill and dying. In August, 430, he died, happily spared the burning of the city which occurred after its fall a year later.

Although Augustine lived twenty years after Alaric took Rome the year 410 was a critical date, the watershed in his spiritual journey. Faced by the knowledge that Christian and non-Christian alike were overwhelmed and dismayed by the threat to the future of civilization implied in the fall of Rome, and knowing full well that many placed the responsibility for the event on the Christians who had persuaded the Emperor to desert the old pagan deities, Augustine sat down to find a solution. The result, which entailed thirteen years of labour (413-26) amidst his episcopal duties was the massive *City of God*. Multifarious in its contents, one resounding theme permeates it, that we are strangers in the world of sense, that our real inheritance is heavenly, that we are pilgrims after perfection. Augustine takes two cities, the city of God (*civitas Dei*) and the earthly city (*civitas terrena*). It is inaccurate to identify the Roman empire with the earthly city, for the earthly city is the city which is based on worldly objects. The Roman empire, like the Christian Church, only more so, stands between the perfect and imperfect orders of existence. The *City of God* placed both in their true context. The heavenly city consisted of the angels as well as of the elect of God. It was characterized by absolute justice, the perfect relationship or order between man and God, of which human justice is but a pale reflection, by perfect law and perfect peace. "Set justice aside", he says in one oft-quoted passage, "then, and what are kingdoms but great robberies? because what are robberies but little kingdoms . . . to war against one's neighbours, and to proceed to the hurt of such as hurts you not, for greedy desire of rule and sovereignty, what is this but flat thievery in a greater excess and quantity than ordinary?'' Peace to Augustine meant a positive state of mind, not the mere absence of war; ''since a man is commanded to love his neighbour as his own self, so much he do for his wife, children, family, and all men besides . . . thus shall he be settled in peace and orderly concord with all the world.'' The heavenly state was thus a universal state bound together by a bond of eternal love. Rising above the crisis of the world, Augustine called men to regard the vision of the eternal transcending and yet immanent within the world of being. ''The main end of this city's aim is either to be called Eternity in peace, or Peace in eternity, and (this) is plain to all.''

If the perfect society may not be identified with the visible Christian Church, this intellectual catharsis had yet made him realize more clearly than ever the necessity for preserving its unity. A more tolerant age than his own in matters of religion may find Augustine's enthusiasm for the combat of heresy puzzling; but heretical action aroused him to vehement response. The ''seamless robe'' of the Church was being split by irresponsible and selfish sectaries; the peace and justice of the city of God were made impossible of achievement in the Catholic Church by the folly of self-centred opinion. ''Why do we not toil together in the one vineyard of our Lord, both alike endeavouring to be wheat and bearing with the worthless grain? Why not, I beseech you, what is the reason? Is any man the better for our divisions? What possible good can it serve? Tell me? Unity is lost, while a people redeemed by the blood of the One Lamb live in angry opposition against each other. Discord exists in that very region where of all others, discord ought to cease. Our Lord said 'First be reconciled unto thy brother and then come and offer thy gift at the Altar'." His own diocese was disturbed by the Donatists, a group of rigid and passionate fanatics who, at the beginning of the fourth century, had condemned the generosity of the Church towards those who in time of persecution were thought to have compromised with the persecuting state. Augustine's arguments were trenchant, but arguments were of little avail with the Donatists; the Council of Carthage (410) which ordered them to return to the Catholic Church only produced a renewal of Donatist fury, particularly when the edict of the Church was confirmed by the emperor. Augustine's experience also proved invaluable in refuting the arguments put forward by his former friends, the Manichaeans. The third group of heretics who challenged the unity of the Church were to Augustine, with his urgent sense of the omnipotence of God and of man's utter helplessness, the most dangerous. A Welshman, Pelagius or Morgan by name, remonstrated with the clergy of Rome for the vices of their city and was told in reply that human weakness made this inevitable. Pelagius thought this attitude profoundly unchristian. Furthermore it seemed to him to spring from Augustine's emphasis on man's total depravity which threw all the apparent onus for man's salvation on to God. In violent reaction he threw all the responsibility on man; "if I ought", summed up his theory, "therefore I can". He was an able and sincere man whose views attracted many adherents, including Pope Zosimus, but he could not outargue Augustine. The latter was convinced, if only by the nature of his own quest for God. Man had so fallen from grace that he could do nothing by his own free will. "After his sin", as he expressed it, "Adam having been driven away from Eden, his entire posterity, which by his sin had been infected and corrupted in himself, as in the stem of the human family, has been included within the bonds of death and of damnation.'' In his reply, Augustine put forward some views which it is difficult to accept; but they influenced the reformers of the sixteenth century profoundly. If Augustine appears a formidable, even an intolerant controversialist, it was because he believed that such controversy was an essential factor in the promotion of the *civitas Dei*. He was torn by sadness as he watched the Church, the visible society of believers, split by division and intrigue. It was because he saw that Christ suffered on the Cross again in the division of the mystical body of the Church, which was steeped in His own blood, that he spent so much time in working for reconciliation.

The tremendous prolificity of Augustine, his sweeping intellectual vitality, the strength of his response to the challenge of his times, lay in his conception of the meaning and measure of the love of God. This was the single, unitary theme which formed both the object of his quest and the method by which it was achieved. It was his unique contribution to theology that he combined the two distinct forms of love, earthly and heavenly; "he lives on", writes Dr. Nygren, "the frontier of two separate religious worlds, those of Hellenistic Eros and primitive Christian Agape, and his significance lies chiefly in the fact that these worlds really meet in his person to form a spiritual unity." Dr. Burnaby suggested in his Hulsean lectures, *Amor Dei,* that there was another important constituent—that of *philia* or friendship. From the very start he had sought love, hungered after love, and sought God through love until the love of God at the last was freely bestowed on him; Agape had transcended and absorbed Eros. "Through the Incarnation we are drawn into the magnetic field of the eternal world and may taste something of the sweetness of the heavenly love."

Worn out by his unceasing labours, Augustine died in a city besieged by barbarians; he might have anticipated the day when the break-up of the irrigation system would turn Rome's granary into a waterless desert and when infidel ships would anchor in the blue bay by which his city stood. He could hardly foresee that no man would so influence future generations as he would. We shall not, indeed, come across his like again. He was a prophetic and awe-inspiring character, throwing down gleams of light over all successive ages. His *Confessions* remain one of the greatest of autobiographies. His emphasis on righteousness, *justitia* formed the foundation on which the Papacy endeavoured to found its moral supremacy in the Middle Ages. The great canonist, Gratian, quoted Augustine 530 times in his *Decretum*. The *City of God* formed the favourite book of the Emperor Charlemagne and of King Louis IX of France. Catholic and Protestant alike have drawn from the well-watered fields of his thought. No man did more "to bring Christian conceptions into touch with philosophical principles", and to permit the marriage of Hellenic tradition and western Catholicism.

It is not strange that this should be so. Faced by the apparent disintegration of society and the prevailing culture, tautened by an intense inward struggle, he acted as the divine response to the challenge of the crisis of his age. He presented a disintegrating civilization with an integrated philosophy of life. He saw things clearly and he saw them whole. If nature was perverse and corrupt, if man had fallen from grace, yet nature and supernature were no less welded together in one unity created out of infinity by God. His works reveal his close interest in nature, in birds and animals, and in natural objects, more, however, as manifestations of divine power, than as objects of scientific experiment. Everything must, in fact, be completely subordinate to the power of God and of His Christ. He knew that the state must be subordinate to the divine law, and that there were some things which the most omnipotent of states could not justly touch. Man's first allegiance is to the city of God, and he may only obey the earthly state as long as its commands are sanctioned by the heavenly society and the divine law. To prevailing frustration and despair, anarchy and lawlessness he posed one sublime and supreme law—"I desire to know God and the soul. Nothing besides? Nothing at all." "From his distant Africa", the French historian, Duchesne, comments, "Augustine shed his light over the whole of Christendom . . . He was the instructor of the whole Middle Ages . . . In certain aspects he is in every age."

But Mr. Gibbon did not agree: "the most conspicuous of his virtues was an ardent zeal against the heretics of every denomination . . . the superficial learning of Augustine was confined to the Latin language; and his style, though sometimes animated by the eloquence of passion, is usually clouded by false and affected rhetoric. But he possessed a strong, capacious, argumentative mind . . ." It was unfortunate, but then Mr. Gibbon, with all his learning and mastery, did not understand Augustine. He could not comprehend sympathetically the intensity of feeling aroused by the supreme crisis which he was recording nor see that Augustine's response to that crisis was supremely relevant to every successive world crisis. In experience and in thought, in prayer and devotion he had, at moments, transcended time: "I desire to know God and the soul. Nothing besides? Nothing at all." No, nothing at all, for all else is comprehended in the one desire. But Mr. Gibbon would not understand.

Books for Further Reading

The Confessions of St. Augustine (Everyman Edition).

The City of God, Introd., by Ernest Barker, 1931.

N. H. Baynes, The Political Ideas of St. Augustine's "De Civitate Dei", 1936.

E. Gilson, Introduction à l'Étude de la Philosophie de St. Augustin, 2nd. ed., 1943.

H. Pope, Saint Augustine of Hippo, 1937.

J. Burnaby, Amor Dei, 1938.

E. Przywara, An Augustine Synthesis, 1936.

Various, A Monument to St. Augustine, 1930.

II. St. Francis of Assisi

THE WORLD of the twelfth century was a splendid world but, more than the Europe of Augustine, it is strange and distant to the modern observer. The society and the culture which it represented was not static; it was full of development and change, penetrated by fast moving themes which gave it colour, feeling and faith. The world of the strip-system of agriculture, of heavy forests, virgates and villeins, and of little market towns was also the scene of a slowly developing political machinery, of an improving agriculture, of cities where the cloth industry was already employing many workers, of a vast spiritual institution whose tentacles gripped all Europe, of newly-hewn stone castles and cathedrals, of scholars and universities. The age was splendid because there was so much that was original and fresh and enthusiastic in it. The consecration of the great Abbey Church of St. Denis in 1140 witnessed the creation of a new style, the Gothic, which embodied "the spiritual desire for a new kind of expression". Thirty-four years later the fire which destroyed the old choir of Canterbury Cathedral gave William of Sens a wonderful opportunity to weave a miracle of stone. The cathedrals of Sens, Noyon, Senlis, Notre Dame at Paris, Laon and Chartres were all begun before 1200. Such new forms in architecture expressed a frame of mind. Faith and spiritual activity were both widening their frontiers. In the works of Abelard it is possible to see a conjunction of faith and reason absent in an earlier age which formed a precursor to the glories of the scholastic school of Chartres. Scholarship

was alive, sparkling, eager. The activity of faith was everywhere manifest, not only in the building of cathedrals
but of churches and monasteries, of crusades and pilgrimages, in the general atmosphere of the period. St. Bernard
of Clairvaux, who died at the middle of the century, was
perhaps the century's most representative figure. Preacher
and statesman of eminence, he was, above all, a reformer
and a mystic, seeking to renew the earlier austerity of
Benedictine monasticism by sweeping away all the secular
fancies and ambitions which blocked the lane of love to
God.

Yet the age was faced by a crisis, not a crisis on a scale
such as that which confronted Augustine eight centuries
earlier, not an economic crisis, even if this also characterized the age and had some part in preparing the way for
Magna Carta, but by a spiritual climacteric. The crisis of
men's minds which came to a peak in the pontificate of one
of the most able of all the popes, Innocent III, was both a
crisis of action and thought. In the past century and a
half the Church had recovered something of the sense of
mission which, except possibly in Ireland, had been largely
forgotten in the Dark Ages—in the mere struggle for
survival. But the approach to power was not without
temptation. The standard of learning and morality among
the ordinary secular clergy was abominably low; council
after council complained of simony, moral irregularities of
every kind, and neglect of duty. Different defects affected
contemporary monasticism. Endowments and security
brought wealth and religious apathy, with the result that
some monks cared more for their lands than their tenants,
more for their stomachs than their minds. Even the great
new abbeys reared by the newly founded Cistercian and
the reformed orders were not wholly immune from these
faults. Less than half a century after their foundation the

meetings of the different Chapters are full of complaints of laxity and abuse. The Cistercians were already on the way to becoming the great sheepfarmers of medieval Europe. The head was almost as afflicted as the body, for the Popes had been involved in the struggle with the Emperor with some loss to their spiritual dignity. The election of Innocent III in 1198 constitutes a landmark, for no pope before or after him had so great a sense of temporal and spiritual responsibility or such an opportunity for carrying it into effect; but his mind was judicial rather than spiritual. He could not give the Church the spiritual stimulus which it required.

The crisis of the last half of the twelfth century also involved thought as well. It was impossible to halt the intellectual rush of man's mind, but there was much in the nature of the advance alarming to the contemporary churchman. The conservative rearguard, headed by Bernard, had done what it could to stamp out the new elements which seemed to challenge the supremacy of faith, but in vain. There was a resurgence of dualism, of that very Manichaeism which had once attracted Augustine, which continued to secure adherents in spite of official condemnation by the Church. The writings of a Moslem philosopher, Averroes, had more serious implications; influenced by reading the works of the ancient Greek philosopher, Aristotle, he put forward a theory of knowledge which challenged the Christian doctrine of God and creation. In an age whose thought had been dominated hitherto by Platonism, distilled through the writings of Augustine, there was a renewed interest in Aristotle which caused great anxiety to churchmen. The Middle Ages was an age of faith, but there were moments in its history when such faith was lacking in stability, and uncertain of direction. Such a period had now occurred.

The crisis of thought was met by Thomas Aquinas, that of action by Francis of Assisi. No two men were so much unalike but they performed a parallel function in the spiritual history of mankind by responding to the challenge of their age. Francis embodied an active Christianity which challenged the standards of the secular and regular clergy of the Church, for he proved that loyalty to the Christ must be absolute. He saw that the approach to God was like an obstacle race in which property constituted the major impediment. He became "possessionless", *il poverello,* the little poor man, simply because possessions had so completely distorted the mission of the Church. Bereft of material obligations, the soul was able to approach close to God through the sheer, soaring music of joy at God's creation. Like Augustine, Francis resolved the crisis of the age in the synthesis of earthly and heavenly love. Max Scheler[1] thus interprets the infinite attraction of Francis' ideal of love: "what really happened was a meeting, altogether singular and unique in its kind, between 'Eros and Agape' . . . in a soul which was originally holy and extraordinary, a meeting which culminated in such an inter-penetration of the two loves that it produced the most extraordinary and sublime example of 'spiritualization of life' and 'vivifying of spirit', which had ever been known."

The small Italian city of Assisi, near to the wooded slopes of the Apennines, formed the background to Francis' early life. The Italy of his day was full of conflict and disorder. Not infrequently, imperial armies marched in the wake of their master, the Emperor. More often the little different city states warred either with each other or were the scene of faction fights between the urban nobility, *the magnati,* and the people, *the popolani.* The peasants or *contadini* who

---

[1] M. Scheler, *Nature et Formes de la Sympathie* cited in M. C. D'Arcy, *The Mind and Heart of Love,* 1945, 232.

disliked the overlordship of the towns were often drawn into the conflict. Francis' father was a cloth merchant, Pietro Bernardone, who was ambitious for his son and had him brought up to speak French. This was important, for French was the language of the wandering troubadours whose romantic tales of love and chivalry seem to have greatly influenced the development of Francis' mind. As far as the evidence goes, the boy's early career was commonplace. He did not, nor ever did, care for learning. He loved to spend his time in merrymaking, extravagance and irresponsible behaviour. It was according to form that at the age of twenty he should have sought to excel in knightly war against Perugia, only to find himself a captive after the skirmish near Ponte San Giovanni in 1202. He was not long in prison but it may be that the enforced inactivity compelled him, as it did Ignatius Loyola at a later date, to think anew, led to an inrush of meditative analysis through which gleams of true spirituality might appear. If this was so, it did not affect his behaviour on his return. And then he fell ill; in the stress of approaching death he realized the nihilism, the meaningless nature of his life. Yet the jolt proved insufficient in itself to lead to a change of conduct. If he knew in his inmost self that life was arid and barren, he tried to evade the issue by losing himself in a renewed search for pleasure and for military honour. He set out on one such expedition, and then returned. Why? No apparent answer is possible, save that his ambition had suddenly deserted him and that his personality was undergoing a profound, radical change.

Francis' conversion was not abrupt. The seeds that had settled in late adolescence took time to mature, and only emerged after an agonizing struggle with their environment. Clearly realizing the tremendous challenge which his religion laid on him, he would have avoided it if he could.

As it was, he could only meet it satisfactorily by a series of actions that strike us as crude and dramatic; but to Francis they represented the admission in practice of what his mind had already admitted to be true. Going as a pilgrim to Rome, he came face to face with a leper and in repulsion changed direction. The change of direction was significant because it was retrogressive. Yet the seeds of spiritual victory were strong enough in him to withstand such a withdrawal. He turned back, gave all the money he possessed to the leper *and* kissed his hand. More than any of his later actions, this was expressive. The young knight had broken through the bounds of contemporary convention by his realization that behind the filthy, deadening scales of the leper there lay a God-created soul. The kiss expressed the victory of love. On his return he spent much time in the half-ruined little chapel at St. Damian, finding in the blinding intensity of his prayer the solution to all his mental wanderings. "Great and glorious God, and thou, Lord Jesus, I pray ye shed abroad your light in the darkness of my mind. . . . Be found of me, Lord, so that in all things I may act in accordance with thy holy will." Believing that Jesus wished him to restore the chapel of St. Damian, he sold the bales of his father's cloth in the market at Foligno and on his return presented the money to the priest to repair the chapel. The horror and anger of Bernardone may be imagined, nor, I think, is it just to think too hardly of him. His violence may be inexcusable, but to see his cherished son fritter time and money away in senseless reverie was bad enough, to witness such folly as he had now seen was madness. A modern psychiatrist might have come to the same conclusion. A young man of comparative wealth and ability had suddenly flung away all his hopes, replaced his fine clothes by rags and had made himself the equal, nay, the inferior, of his inferiors. Even the children of Assisi thought of him as a madman, "un pazzo". Francis' action was extravagant, eccentric but it was not insane. When his father finally called on Bishop Guido to intervene, he appeared stark naked in the bishop's presence and handed his entire possessions to the bishop with the words: "Listen, all of you, and understand it well; until this time I have called Pietro Bernardone my father, but now I desire to serve God. This is why I return to him this money, for which he has given himself so much trouble, as well as my clothing, and all that I have had from him, for from henceforth I desire to say nothing else than 'Our Father, which art in heaven'." This was not madness; it was a delirious acceptance of reality, the emotional and intellectual triumph which came after months of weary struggle. The final note was uttered on St. Matthias' Day, 1208, in the little church of the Portiuncula where Francis was assisting as a deacon (he was never, incidentally, ordained priest) at Mass. The words of the Gospel struck him with uncontrollable force: "Wherever ye go, preach saying 'The kingdom of heaven is at hand. Heal the sick, cleanse the lepers, cast out devils; freely ye have received, freely give. Provide neither gold nor silver nor brass in your purses, nor scrip for your journey, nor two coats, nor shoes nor staff; for the labourer is worthy of his hire'." This formed, as Francis realized, the foundation of an ideal which he endeavoured in the remaining seventeen years of his life to put into practice.

It is difficult to form a connected history of the next few years; they register a series of impressions which gradually create a pattern. Soon after Francis arrived to make the Portiuncula his headquarters, he began to think in terms of a small group which might lead with him the life he had chosen. He had no intention of forming a monastic order, still less of living a life isolated from the remainder of the community. No man saw more clearly that it was only too possible to live outside the world by living completely within it. Gradually the numbers of his disciples grew—first, a rich and well-known citizen of Assisi, Bernardo di Quintavalle and then others. Their lives were hard and spent in begging for food, in sleeping where they could, in preaching simple sermons, in doing acts of kindness, especially towards the lepers, but their joy was as fresh and as colourful as the almond-blossom on the trees in spring. There were many moments of difficulty, for there were some who misunderstood them and others, especially among the clergy, who distrusted them and thought that they might be heretics like the Cathari of Southern France. Yet Francis' attraction was irresistible. More and more friars were drawn to his fervent devotion and warmed by the very simplicity of his teaching: "Let us consider," he said, "that God in his goodness has not called us merely for our own salvation, but also for that of many men, that we may go through all the world exhorting men, more by our example than by our words, to repent of their sins and bear the commandments in mind."

In the summer of 1210, Francis again made his way to Rome in order that he might secure the approval of Innocent III for the rule of life which he had made. This was extremely simple, being founded on passages from the Scriptures. There was the very greatest difference in the world between the young, swarthy but delicate friar and the cultured, legally-minded Pope. Well aware of the evils which were afflicting his times, and yet, despite the judicial nature of his mind, careful for the things of the soul (as the books which he had written before his election to the pontificate reveal), Innocent trod warily. He knew that the Church had been harmed before by ardour without discretion, nor could he know of the light of love which illumined Francis. "My dear children," he told the friars, "your life appears to me too severe; I see indeed that your fervour is too great for any doubt of you to be possible, but I ought to consider those who shall come after you, lest your mode of life should be beyond their strength." Considering the future history of the Franciscans, these were wise words, but even Innocent could not long withstand the urgent appeal of *il poverello*. Without yet giving them a rule, he expressed the keenest approbation for their work and approved their missionary activity.

Are the years that follow an anti-climax? Certainly Francis and his companions lived a more strenuous life than ever. "The whole country trembled, the barren land was already covered with a rich harvest, the withered vines began again to blossom." From their headquarters at Rivo-Torto the friars conducted preaching missions in the neighbouring towns and villages and, as they increased in numbers, wandered further afield in Italy. In 1212 Francis made his first attempt to preach the gospel to the infidels. The twelfth century had been the great age of the crusades, the armed forces which tried to oust the Saracens from Jerusalem with the blessing of the Church. The motives which impelled the crusaders to take their vows were frequently inspired by desire for economic and political gain, as the crusade of 1204 revealed, but the sublime romance of the crusading ideal continued to attract many, among whom Francis may be counted. His first attempt failed nor was an attempt which he made to reach the Spanish Moors, recently defeated at the great battle of Las Navas de Tolosa, more successful. Seven years later, Francis and other friars accompanied the crusaders to Damietta. It is improbable that they made any impression on the Saracen, for they did not know the language nor did they understand the immense nature of the task. It is more certain that they created a great impression amongst the crusading armies themselves; such is the witness of a contemporary, Jacques de Vitry. He wrote that Francis had preached before the sultan and that many of his own companions had joined the "Order of the Brothers Minor, an Order which is multiplying rapidly on all sides, because it imitates the primitive Church and follows the life of the Apostles in everything. The master of these Brothers is named Brother Francis; he is so lovable that he is venerated by everyone". But the main work of the order lay in Europe. The general chapter of 1217 reflects the vast expansion of their work; Italy and other European countries were each grouped into provinces under the control of a provincial minister. France, Germany, Spain and Portugal, England (the first English house was founded by Agnellus of Pisa in 1224) all formed the scene of their preaching missions.

Such expansion brought with it new problems with which Francis' saintly personality was not well suited to deal. His life was like an arrow directed from a shaft at the bull's eye of a target, the unstained, luminous love of God. Urgently aware as he was of the power of sin and temptation, he yet felt the transcendent love of God in creation so strongly that he could hardly visualize the weakness of some of his own followers. It was his one concession to the austerity of existence that he allowed the friars to leave one strip of the garden for flowers that they might reflect God's glory. The famous incident of the birds at Bavagna which in any other saint might seem senti-mental is so absolutely in character that it must have some foundation in truth. "Brother birds you ought to praise and love your Creator very much. He has given you feathers for clothing, wings for flying, and all that is needful for you. He has made you the noblest of his creatures; he permits you to live in the pure air; you have neither to sow nor to reap, and yet He takes care of you, watches over you and guides you." This was, however, obviously not the type of mind which could grapple with the intricacies of administration. It was the freedom of the spirit rather than the rule of the law which Francis sought. It is not surprising that he looked on the attempts to define and expand the rule with scarcely concealed anxiety. "My brethren", he told the Chapter, "the Lord called me by the way of simplicity and humility and showed me this way of life in truth, for me and for others who will believe and imitate me. Wherefore I will not have you name unto me any other Rule, whether of St. Benedict or St. Augustine or St. Bernard; nor any other form of life except this which the Lord in his mercy hath shown and given unto me." But the protector of the Order of Friars, the aged Cardinal Ugolino, who undoubtedly had a genuine devotion to the founder, thought otherwise. There is little point in detailing the crisis which led eventually to the formation of a rule in 1223. The rule insisted on the observance of absolute poverty and stressed the duty of work, but it seems clear that Francis' later years were clouded by forebodings for the future. "Lord Jesus . . . thou hast raised up the Religion of the Brothers in order to uphold faith, and that by them the mystery of thy gospel may be accomplished. Who will take their place if, instead of fulfilling their mission and being shining examples for all, they are seen to give themselves up to works of darkness? Oh, may they be accursed by thee, Lord, and by all the court of heaven, and by me, thine unworthy servant, they who by their bad example overturn and destroy all that thou didst do in the beginning and ceasest not to do by the holy Brothers of this Order."

There was no relaxation of energy in the saint's closing years, but the unceasing labour, the constant preaching and journeying, the austere manner of life, had worn out the body long before its time. It seems probable that he had long been suffering from tuberculosis, a fever which often sharpens the imagination and heightens the spiritual perceptions. Francis was more and more taken up with the self-identification of his personality with that of the Christ through the suffering and joy of love. In 1224 he went to Laverna, a rocky hill in Casentino cloaked by beech trees and tall pines which had been given to him by a local landowner, Count Orlando. Here on the feast of the Elevation of the Holy Cross (September 14th) he received the Stigmata, the imprint, like fleshy excrescences, of the wounds that Christ endured on the Cross. If, like C. S. Lewis, we were to judge the miraculous by our "innate sense of the fitness of things", nothing was more appropriate in Francis' life than the Stigmata. Yet its occurrence does not affect the vitality and poetry of his faith, at this time revealed in the touching Canticle of the Sun. The constant hæmorrhages proved more and more exhausting, revealing to Francis that death was near. "Father," said a doctor from Arezzo, "this will all pass away, if it pleases God." "I am not a cuckoo," the saint replied, "to be afraid of death. By the grace of the Holy Spirit I am so intimately united to God that I am equally content to live or to die." They removed him from the Bishop's palace to Portiuncula where, on October 3rd, 1226, he embraced death. On Sunday, July 26th, 1228, Pope Gregory IX—the former Cardinal Ugolino—arrived at Assisi to perform the stately ceremonial of canonization.

It is at this point that one would wish the characters to appear, as in T. S. Eliot's *Murder in the Cathedral,* to detail their arguments as to whether the Franciscan movement betrayed its founder or whether, as Paul Sabatier insisted, the spiritual loveliness of Francis was imprisoned in an ecclesiastical institution. It is certain that the Catholic Church, with that sureness of vision which so often distinguishes it, made a master-stroke in attaching the friars to the Pope, but there is no reason to suppose that Francis ever considered any other alternative. It is much more to the point that Francis' emphasis on the divine nature of poverty was neglected; "we are accustomed", wrote Dr. A. G. Little, a masterly interpreter of the Franciscan movement, "to think of a poor man as one who lacks riches; St. Francis thought of a rich man as one who lacked the inestimable boon of poverty". The early Franciscans kept as closely as they could to their founder's ideal; "such was his zeal for poverty", wrote Thomas of Eccleston of the first English provincial, Agnellus of Pisa, "that he would scarcely permit any ground to be enlarged or houses to be built unless unavoidable". By comparison with the other orders, the Franciscans certainly held relatively little land in England, but gradually both "usus laxus" (i.e. "poverty without penury") and "usus pauper" (real poverty) disappeared. Forbidden to touch or purchase money, they made use of a third person, a spiritual friend, who before the middle of the thirteenth century had, in effect, become a business agent. Signs of increasing material comfort soon made themselves felt; in shoes and tunics of better quality,[1] in improved food; even begging began to be systematized. There was also a conflict between the friars and the parish priests who were jealous of the former's popularity and their claim to preach, to hear confessions and to bury secular persons in their churches. This problem was finally regulated by the papal bull, *Super Cathedram,* but the whole question left an unpleasant taste in the mouth, completely

---

[1] Cf. the author of *Pierce the Ploughman's Crede:*

"That in cotynge of his cope is more cloth y folden
Than was in Fraunces froc when he hem first made."

alien to the spirit of Francis. Chaucer has left an inimitable picture of the friar who

> "*In every hous he gan to poure and prye,*
> *And beggeth mele, and chese, or elles corn.*
> *His felawe hadde a staf tipped with horn,*
> *A peyre of table al of yvory,*
> *And a poyntel*[1] *polisshed fetisly*[2]
> *And wroot thy names alway, as he stood,*
> *Of alle folk that yaf him any good,*
> *Ascaunces*[3] *that he wolde for hem preye,*
> '*Yeve us a busshel whete, malt or reye*
> *A goddes*[4] *kechil,*[5] *or a trip*[6] *of chese;*
> *A godes half-peny or a masse-peny,*
> *Or yeve us of your brawn, if ye have eny*
> *A dagon*[7] *of your blanket, leve dame,*
> *Our suster dere, lo! here I write your name;*
> *Bacon or beef or swich thing as ye finde*'."

A group of Franciscans, known as the Fraticelli or the Spiritual Franciscans, kept faithfully to the rigid rule of their founder, which his great friend and imitator, St. Clare, maintained until her death in 1254. They held that it was incumbent upon every follower of Francis to live in absolute poverty. There were poets like Jacopone da Todi and mystics like Gerardo di San Donnino among their number. Unfortunately, it was not only their poverty which made them suspect at the luxurious papal court at Rome and later at Avignon. They were tainted with heresy, with preaching the emergence of a spiritual Church which would replace the mundane contemporary Church. And Joachim of Flora had long ago prophesied that the age of nettles would in

---

[1] style for writing.   [3] as if.   [5] small cake.   [7] small piece.
[2] exquisitely.   [4] God's.   [6] small piece.

turn give way to the age of roses and the age of lilies, to the consummation of the Holy Spirit. Such views procured their persecution and eventual condemnation by Pope John XXII. But all was not lost. In 1334 Friar Giovanni Valle received permission to found a hermitage near Foligno which led to the rise of the Friars of the Strict Observance who, as far as possible, maintained Francis' original austerity. The personality of Francis was never in the days of greatest abuse entirely lost sight of. We see the Franciscans at Gloucester with "bees, cord, teazles, onions and apples" or at Shrewsbury with a "walnoot orchard", or travelling in far-off lands as missionaries and preachers. Even though Francis, as an unlearned man, suspected learning, they adorned scholarship in the persons of St. Bonaventure, Alexander of Hales, Roger Bacon and Duns Scotus. The splendid flame of Francis' faith and charity continued to inspire the grey friars everywhere. In his charming pen-picture of the saint, G. K. Chesterton wrote: "The figure in the brown habit stands above the hearth in the room where I write, and alone among many such images, at no stage of my pilgrimage has never seemed to be a stranger. There is something of harmony between the hearth and the firelight and my own first pleasure in his words about his brother fire; for he stands far enough back in my memory to mingle with all those more domestic dreams of the first days. . . . His figure stands on a sort of bridge connecting my boyhood with my conversion to many other things." Such has been the experience of many.

What then is the final verdict? Whatever the future of the Franciscan order, whatever the betrayal of Francis' own ideals, he had resolved the challenge of the times by recalling in his person the Christ whom he loved so dearly. What the contemporary Church required was a man who would reveal a standard of conduct to which it could aspire even if it could not reach it, and which might represent yet another renunciation of evil. Francis was indeed the spring of a reform movement in the lives of men and women everywhere. In some ways he was the father of the great medieval missionary movement. He certainly released new energy and drive, a new sense of piety and the poetry of life, of vitality and infectious enthusiasm, which refreshed and revivified men and women. He had met the challenge of his own age and, despite the sadness which sometimes marred his joy, had overcome it. But this is not all. His radiant personality is a mirror for all ages, the mirror of the man who cut himself so loose from all ties that he might serve man to enjoy God. Let G. K. Chesterton have the last word: "He went out half-naked in his hair-shirt into the winter woods, walking the frozen ground between the frosty trees, a man without a father. He was penniless, he was parentless . . . he burst suddenly into song." And the song resounded throughout Europe. "God Almighty, eternal, righteous and merciful," he told his brothers, "give to us poor wretches to do for thy sake all that we know of thy will, and to will always what pleases thee; so that inwardly purified, enlightened and kindled by the fire of the Holy Spirit, we may follow in the footprints of thy well-beloved Son our Lord Jesus Christ."

<h2>BOOKS FOR FURTHER READING</h2>

The Mirror of Perfection (Ascribed to Leo of Assisi), Eng. trans., S. Evans, 1898.

The Little Flowers of St. Francis, Eng. trans., T. W. Arnold, 1908.

Life of St. Francis, Thomas of Celano, Eng. trans., A. G. Ferrers Howell, 1908.

P. Sabatier, *St. Francis of Assisi*, Eng. trans., L. S. Houghton, 1894.

Fr. Cuthbert, *St. Francis of Assisi*, 1912.

A. G. Little, *A Guide to Franciscan Studies*, 1920.

A. G. Little, *St. Francis of Assisi*, 1912.

A. G. Little, *Studies in English Franciscan History*, 1917.

G. K. Chesterton, *St. Francis of Assisi*, 1923.

St. Francis of Assisi, Essays in Commemoration, 1926.

G. G. Coulton, *St. Bernard and St. Francis*, 1932.

D. C. Douie, *The Nature and Effect of the Theory of the Fraticelli*, 1932.

J. R. H. Moorman, *Sources for the life of St. Francis*, 1941.

J. R. H. Moorman, *The New Fioretti*, 1946.

c

III. St. Thomas Aquinas

THE CRISIS of the twelfth-century Church was intellectual as well as moral, for the pulsating, lively mind of the contemporary scholar found that the traditions which had been acceptable to his fathers no longer met his own requirements. Current scholarship at the beginning of the twelfth century owed most to the thought of St. Augustine of Hippo and through him to Plato, but it was challenged from two directions. In the first place there were thinking men who held that too much dependence was placed on faith and that too little attention was paid to man's reason; such was one opinion of the French theologian, Abelard, who made a greater use of the dialectical method than his contemporaries. The achievements of their own age, the massive, cool, pillared naves of the newly built cathedrals, the manuscripts and learning of the monasteries, the growth of the universities, made them respect the work of man's mind and led them to think that God could not have intended that man should depend on revelation alone. Man's reasoning powers might lead him towards divine truth. There was then a tendency among the more advanced thinkers of the day to contrast the degree of knowledge attained through the use of man's reasoning powers with the certainty of faith which he gained through revelation. Although there were conservatives who condemned the development as unduly arrogant and dangerous, ecclesiastical authority, on the whole, approved the trend of modern scholarship had it not been for a further development which was really alarming.

This was the rediscovery of the works of Plato's pupil, Aristotle, distributed to Europe through the medium of the Spanish and Sicilian translators. The greater part of southern Spain was a Moslem State where culture, learning and cleanliness flourished among the orange groves and delicately trellised courts of the emirs. Two Arabic writers of great brilliance, Avicenna and Averroes, made themselves the foremost interpreters of the work of Aristotle to the western world. The rediscovery of the "philosopher", as later writers in the Middle Ages called him, might seem to be singularly unalarming, especially as he was known to be a pupil of the other great Pagan writer, Plato, to whom contemporary thought owed a great deal. But this was not the point. The Platonic and Neoplatonic tradition was already challenged. The teachings of Averroes, passing into Europe through his pupil, Siger of Brabant, challenged it still more and endangered Christian theology itself by revealing that Aristotle held views about fundamental Christian matters, individuality, freedom, immortality, providence, and the eternity of the world, which were not in harmony with Christian teaching. Furthermore, there was a great vogue for Aristotle's works among the more lively minds of the day who, passing as they did from university to university, were in the position of being able to spread them throughout all the cultural centres of Europe. Averroes, for instance, held that God was a being self-existent in contemplation, which at once removed Him from the realm of Christian thought and made nonsense of the Incarnation. There was a real danger that the ecclesiastical authorities would take fright and condemn the reading of Aristotle's works outright, as indeed they did in 1210 at Corbeil; mainly because they challenged the essentials of faith. If they had done this, they would have driven a cleft stick into the intellectual life of the time, dividing the world of scholarship into those who held that knowledge was ultimately a question of faith and those who held that it was primarily a matter of reason. The disastrous consequences of this kind of approach to thought and life were well revealed in the later Middle Ages as in more modern times. If the mysteries of life were to be apprehended they could only be understood if they were viewed as a whole. There was a real danger in the ferment of the intellectual world of the time that the obscurantists might triumph, simply because progressive thought seemed and actually was dangerous.

It was Thomas Aquinas who not only reconciled the Platonism of the past with the Aristotelianism of the present but also brought them both within the Christian philosophy of life. His thought was not outstandingly original. It was gloriously clear, for he was a consummate master of analysis and synthesis. He married faith and reason together in a marvellous unity and so resolved the doubts of conservatives and progressives in the finest compromise the world has been privileged to see. But compromise and synthesis did not mean, as it might appear, intellectual timidity. Aquinas criticized the neoplatonic thought of one of his contemporaries, the noble St. Bonaventure, and shocked many by asserting that it was impossible to prove by reason that the world had a beginning. And then he turned on Siger of Brabant and equally shocked the left-wing of scholastic thought in the university city of Paris. It is relevant to recall that the age of the *Summa Theologica* of Thomas was also the age of cathedral building when French Gothic, with its characteristic balance of high tensions, reached its consummation, that, five years before Aquinas' birth, the foundations of the two lovely cathedrals of Amiens and Salisbury were laid; Thomas' thought mirrored the same tendencies as the buildings of the great age. Although each of the buildings merged into the unity of the spire or tower, they were still architecturally a "sum of added units" rather than a single whole. And this was equally true of Thomas' work. His *Summa* was not an original compilation but a massive collection of thought and ideas already in existence, grouped together, analysed, synthetized and integrated by the dominating *motif* of divine love, the spire of thought which gave meaning and life to the whole. The word which best described Thomas' great achievement is, in fact, the architectural word "architectonic". He was the great architect of the age who repaired the battered buildings and gave them vitality and expression and meaning.

The events of Thomas' life have not the supremely moving interest of those of Augustine or Francis, but in their own way reveal that once at least in his career he was faced with a decision of tremendous personal significance. His father was an Italian baron, Laudolf, Count of Aquino, descended from the imperial family, and his mother was of Norman descent. He was born in 1225 or 1226 at the family castle of Roccasicca near Naples. Even in his earliest days, at the local Benedictine Abbey of Monte Cassino, he appears to have shown an overwhelming acute interest in matters divine, asking continually "What is God?" From Monte Cassino he went to the University of Naples where he discovered that the answer to the question which had so long eluded him lay in life's work—or indeed in eternity's work. It was the one answer to which all else must be subordinated. He decided to enter the Dominicans, the order of friars founded by Francis' contemporary, Dominic, for the purpose of teaching people about the Christian faith, and was sent as a pupil to the Dominicans in Paris. It was now that Thomas was faced by the decision on which the remainder of his life depended. His family were horrified by his decision to become a friar, an order of men distinguished indeed for sanctity of life but inappropriate for the scion of such a noble house as that of the lords of Aquino. It is improbable that Thomas said much to their recriminations, he was never given to much talking, but Thomas' silence was more alarming than other people's obstinacy. His two brothers seized him as he was starting on his travels and kept him a prisoner for a year in the castle of San Giovanni. A year of enforced meditation may well have enriched Aquinas' spiritual and mental qualities and certainly gave strength to his decision to become a Dominican friar. Eventually, he reached Paris where he came under the influence of the great teacher, Albert of Cologne. He remained deeply indebted to Albert, for it was he who had first attempted to reconcile Christian thought with Aristotelian philosophy. The immense series of commentaries which he wrote on Aristotle's works provided the groundwork for Thomas' conclusions, but it is clear that the conclusion was Thomas' work alone. Nevertheless, the close companionship of the two men, more particularly as Thomas early became mature, was of vital consequence if only because the interaction of their minds made for greater efficiency of thought. Graduating in 1248, he went with Albert to Cologne and stayed with him as lecturer in the Studium Generale which Albert ran in the city. Four years later he returned to Paris and worked for the degree of Master of Theology, which he received in 1256. He was already well-known as one of the most distinguished of university scholars and was shortly afterwards recalled to Italy. With the exception of a few visits to other countries, to London for a meeting of a general chapter of the Dominicans in 1263 and two years in Paris in 1269–71 to rebut charges made against his philosophy, he spent the remainder of his life in Italy, in writing, in teaching, and

in educational administration. The condemnation of
Averroes' views by the Bishop of Paris in 1270 was very
largely the result of the incisive exposure which Aquinas
had made of them on his visit to the French capital. He
refused all preferment for he knew that this would deflect
him from fulfilling the true object of his labours, and also
because he was a genuinely humble man. In 1274, Pope
Gregory X invited him to attend the general council of the
Church which was meeting at Lyons to discuss the re-
union of the Roman and Greek branches of the Catholic
Church. But he was taken sick and died at the Cistercian
abbey of Fossanuova, near Terracina, on March 7th,
1274.

The "Angelic Doctor", as he was nicknamed, was only
forty-eight when he died. When one considers the
limitations under which any scholar was bound to work in
his days, his output in its range, depth and mastery was
colossal. Quite apart from the *Summa Contra Gentiles* and
the *Summa Theologica,* he wrote many other works on
theology, the religious life and exegesis, some twenty books
on philosophy, and twelve commentaries on Aristotle. The
Summa Theologica, which was incomplete at the time of his
death, alone contains three parts, thirty-eight treatises, six
hundred and thirty-one questions and about three thousand
articles. He was essentially the scholar-saint. His silence
earned him the title of "Dumb Ox" at which Albert (who
died six years after his pupil) appropriately remarked: "You
call him a dumb ox; I tell you this dumb ox shall bellow so
loud that his bellowing will fill the world." He was ox-
like in frame as well as in speech, as medieval pictures
reveal, but his size was not a result of over-eating. He was
so much concerned with prayer and teaching that he had
little time for food or sleep. If his huge size was caused
by the under-activity of his pituitary gland, there was

compensation in the over-activity of the mind. His exceptional powers of concentration enabled him, we are told, to dictate to several secretaries at the same time, but all this completely pales into insignificance by contrast with the rich storehouse of his mind which was so clearly reflected in a series of massive volumes.

His two great books constitute a summary of the whole Christian faith. The *Summa Contra Gentiles* is written to confront unbelievers with a Christian philosophy of existence. The *Summa Theologica* was an ordered exposition of the faith, which he began in 1269; it contains three parts, the first treating of God, His Unity, and His Threefold Personality. The second part, which is divided into two sections, deals with the Word of God and Ethics. The last, unfinished part contains treatises on the Incarnation and the Sacraments. The character of the book is dry and unemotional but its clarity and reasonableness are unsurpassed. It has no high lights or purple passages nor did Thomas permit himself to let loose the feeling which is active in his lovely hymns, *Lauda Sion, Verbum Supernum* and *Pange Lingua*. It is, perhaps, this masterly restraint which gives the *Summa* its eternal value, since its appeal was and must be primarily to the intellect. The method of approach to each problem is logical and dispassionate. Each of the parts which make up the whole is divided into a number of questions (*Quaestiones*) introduced by a statement dealing with the relevance and importance of the issue under discussion. Each question in its turn consists of articles which includes, first, a series of objections to the truth put forward in the article, then a statement of the Biblical or Patristic authorities on which the article is based, followed by Thomas' own views on the problem, and finally a detailed reply to the objections. The whole is set out in a singularly objective and fair fashion.

It would be impossible to do justice in a short essay to the detail of Thomas' arguments, but certain essential factors may be noticed. The *Summa* was, in the first instance, a finely developed synthesis of faith and reason. All knowledge, he said, came from two sources, divine revelation and the human intellect, each being, in the long run, interdependent on the other. The human intellect could not bring its ideas to fruition without the further knowledge provided by faith, which faith could not be understood or properly interpreted without the human mind. "It is impossible", said Thomas, "for the natural reason to arrive at the knowledge of the divine persons. By natural reason we may know those things which pertain to the unity of the divine persons, but . . . he who attempts to prove by the natural reason the trinity of persons, detracts from the rights of faith." But reason is supreme in the world of sense and feeling and can itself prove the existence of God. Philosophy is then the active help-mate of Theology. Theology has the last word, is the queen of the sciences, but is none the less helpless without the assistance of philosophy. "The light of reason within us is able to show us good things, and guides our will, in so far as it is the light of Thy countenance. It is therefore evident that the goodness of the human will depends on the eternal law much more than on the human reason, and when therefore human reason fails we must have recourse to the Eternal Reason."

But the human reason points to the existence of God. Thomas saw far more clearly than most men have done, that this was the fundamental point in Christian philosophy —*if* God exists. If he does not exist then all the tremendous problems raised about his character and his nature and his care and love for men are entirely and hopelessly irrelevant. The essential question upon which all else depends was the answer to this question: "Does God exist?" Thomas held that this was a problem upon which man's own reason could throw a revealing light. More than a century earlier, Anselm had taught that "that than which no greater can be conceived cannot exist only in the understanding", simply because its existence in the mind implies that it must also exist in reality. St. Thomas criticized this on the grounds that because we are bound to think of God existing, by the very nature of the thought which comes into our minds, that is no proof that God exists. In the *Summa* he offered the reader five other proofs of God's existence. There was, first, the argument derived from motion or change which owes much to Aristotle. Thomas asserted that everything which moves must owe its motion to something else or, to put it theologically, all motion or change represents the transformation of what is potentially there into actuality. It is impossible to think of an infinite regress. There must, therefore, be a Prime Mover which causes the movement of all the others but is itself unmoved. "It is necessary to arrive at a First Mover, put into action by no other; and this everyone understands to be God." The second proof is very similar to the first, but is connected with causation rather than motion. Everything is caused by something else, nor is it possible to contemplate an infinite regress since you cannot remove a cause without moving an effect, and thus break the chain of causation. It is, therefore, necessary to predicate a First Cause which is uncaused and yet causes everything else which is God. The third proof partakes of the nature of the other two but is principally concerned with contingency. There are in the world of men many things which are unnecessary and which, being liable to generation and decay, come into existence and later pass away. But this is not true of all beings, for if it were it would mean that there was historically a moment when nothing existed. If nothing existed, nothing could exist, simply because nothing can give rise to nothing. By the same argument, there are, therefore, some things which are necessary but their necessity is not self-existent. They trace their origin to a Prime Necessity which must be called God.

The two last arguments are slightly different in character. Of two things or ideas or attributes presented to us, we say that one is truer than the other and that one is falser than the other, but such a judgment is more than relative. When we say that a thing is false or true, fine or noble, ugly or beautiful, we refer it to a supreme truth, beauty or goodness. As Aristotle said, the truer a thing is, the more it *is*, i.e. the more it is likely to exist. So that which most *is*, is God. The final argument is that based on purpose. An intelligent being acts because it has some final end, apart from the relative objects which shape much of its life. Indeed, if there is a relative object it must be related to a final object, that final object constituting the first Purpose of man. The governance of the world by God is another proof of His existence.

How do these five proofs stand up to modern thought? There are, of course, many difficulties which an intelligent reader would be bound to surmount before he could accept St. Thomas' arguments in their entirety. All the arguments, except the last, depend upon recognizing that an infinite regress is a definite impossibility. That is, you cannot say that A is caused by B, B is caused by C, C is caused by D, without coming sooner ~r later to a final term. Bertrand Russell replies to this that "every mathematician knows that there is no such impossibility; the series of negative integers ending with minus one is an instance to the contrary".[1] On the other hand, Mr.

[1] *History of Western Philosophy*, 1946, 484.

Mascall in an admirable appreciation of the relativity of Thomas' arguments for the existence of God to the modern world, points out that Russell's position "depends upon the axiom that the number of things in the world is infinite (cf. *Intro. to Math. Phil.,* Ch. xiii), an axiom which logicians are by no means unanimous in accepting. (Cf. M. Black, *Nature of Mathematics,* p. 104 f.)"[1] Whatever the logical or philosophical postulates underlying the argument, Thomas Aquinas had made a singularly important contribution to religious philosophy by insisting that the existence of God is essentially reasonable and that man could attain to a knowledge of divine truths through his mind. Man could safely assume that there was an "innate fitness" about the existence of God which his reason proved.

Thomas had also much to say about the meaning of man, who is the creature of God. He insists that man is both body and soul (which is created afresh with every man and gives life to the body) but the soul, unlike the body, is immortal. Man was not primarily created to live the good life but to praise and worship the creator; the good life is an essential factor in such praise and worship. Aquinas pays considerable attention to man's final end, but he always returns to the truth—that God is the alpha and omega of man's desire. In his argument, he is much influenced by Aristotle who had insisted that happiness is the crown of man's existence. He would agree with this but, as always, he enlarges on Aristotle's view and shows that what was lacking in it was an awareness of the Christian philosophy of existence. Temporal happiness is only an immediate end, in itself dependent on and subordinate to man's search for future blessedness. His account of man's final purpose embodies a great deal of his argument: "Now if we wish to assign an end to any whole, and to the parts

[1] *He Who Is,* 1943, 48 n.

of that whole, we shall find, firstly, that each and every part exists for the sake of its proper act, as the eye for the act of seeing; secondly, that less honourable parts exist for the more honourable, as the senses for the intellect, the lungs for the heart; and thirdly, that all parts are for the perfection of the whole, as the matter for the form, for the parts are, as it were, the matter of the whole. Furthermore, the whole man is on account of an extrinsic end, that end being the function of God. So, therefore, in the parts of the universe also every creature exists for its own proper act and perfection, and the less noble for the nobler, as those creatures that are less noble than man exist for the sake of man, whilst each and every creature exists for the perfection of the entire universe. Furthermore, the entire universe, with all its parts, is ordained towards God as the end, inasmuch as it imitates, as it were, and shadows forth the divine goodness, to the glory of God. Reasonable creatures, however, have in some special and higher manner God as their end, since they can attain to him by their own operations of knowing and loving him. Thus it is plain that the Divine Goodness is the end of all corporeal things."

The shadow of eternity governed Thomas' attitude towards secular authority and the state. He agreed with Aristotle that the state is natural to man, and is therefore essential to man's spiritual as well as his moral development. "Hence also Augustine says: just men bear empire not from love of dominion, but from duty to others' welfare" and "this is prescribed by the natural order; God willed it so when he made man". But he also recognized what Aristotle did not, that the validity of the state's authority depended on its incorporation into the framework of eternal law. His theory of law is indeed one of the most important aspects of his teaching. There is, he asserts, a natural law which is unchangeable and of universal validity. It has its source in the eternal reason of God. "The natural law is nothing else than the share of the rational creature in the eternal law." The eternal law is God's law in the sense that all creatures, angels, animals, indeed the whole of creation animate and inanimate, are bound to obey it, but its operation is different in the realm of rational creatures from that of the irrational creation. Although it is dangerous to transfer metaphysical to physical concepts, it is clear that in irrational creation the eternal law constitutes what the scientist means today by natural law. But with man it is different. Man has a mind which can comprehend the eternal law by his own efforts and the grace of God and if he wills, can fulfil it. Just as he is hindered by the power of sin he is assisted to fulfil the law by the human law of the state and the divine law of the church, both imperfect representations of the eternal law. Both are clearly subordinate to the eternal law and in fact only retain their validity in so far as they are in perfect accord with it. A subject's allegiance to authority can therefore never be unconditional because there may be circumstances when his understanding of the rule of law compels his disobedience. "Man is bound to obey the secular rulers in so far as the order of justice requires. Therefore, if they have not a just title, but a usurped one, or if they command what is unjust, their subjects are not bound to obey them; unless perhaps *per accidens* for the avoidance of scandal or of danger." Perforce, the restriction on secular authority is chiefly a matter not for the individual but the institution which guards his rights under the divine law, the Church. The world, he says in one of his rare metaphorical passages, is like a ship in which the secular authority is represented by the carpenter who keeps the ship seaworthy and the church by the pilot who steers it to its destination. "It may well be the task of one man to preserve it (i.e. the ship) in its present state of being, and of another to conduct it to a higher perfection." "The carpenter has the task of repairing any damage which may occur in the ship, while the helmsman has the responsibility of conducting the ship to its port."

Man lives continually then under the impulse of his final objective, the city of God. He may have learned of God's existence by his reason, but reason is crowned by revelation, by the redemption and crucifixion of Christ consummated in the resurrection which reveals the attributes of the Creator and the power of divine love. It is indeed this to which we turn at the last, for nothing else in effect gave so much power and strength to the Dominican's will. What had Thomas to say of love? He rises, although there are some scholars who would deny this, from the lower, human type of love to the divine archetype or *caritas*. Starting from Aristotle he concludes that "Love is something which appertains to desire", that man's greatest desire is to love God, and that "the end of love is beatitude". This is, of course, to approach the whole problem of love from the human end but there are clear signs that he is able to reconcile the two natures of love in a single unity. Each man is a member of the community. As a man, he is intent on serving his own good, on pursuing his own desire. As a member of the community, he serves the good of other people first. In every conflict between man as an individual and man as a member of the community, the membership of the community has an overriding claim. The part is, in fact, less the whole. So it is with man and love for God. "We see that (in a whole) each part by a natural tendency works for the good of the whole, even to its own risk and harm . . . hence every creature in its own way naturally loves God more than it does itself, non-living bodies by their very nature, brute beast sensitively, but a rational creature by intellectual desire, which is called love."[1] But it would be wrong to estimate Thomas' own power of love by the intellectual discussion which he provides in his writings. Thomas' own life was, in itself, an incarnation of service which could only flow freely from love that looked essentially God-ward. From the day when he had told his angry family of his decision to become a Dominican friar to the day when he put away his *Summa Theologica* unfinished, he had spent his mind and spirit in the service of the loving God. The *Summa* was left incomplete partly because death intervened and partly because, as he told a friend who pressed him to continue with his work, "I cannot; such things have been revealed to me that what I have written seems but straw." He had, in fact, experienced the very *amor dei* besides which the massive *Summa* itself appeared unimportant and worthless.

St. Thomas' arguments had, of course, their weaknesses. His search for reason only took place within a framework of passionate belief. It was neither impartial nor completely logical. He was like a man who lived in a valley and saw a high mountain but he could not at first descry the best path. He never for one moment doubted the existence of the mountain and yet he knew that if he could but find the path he would realize how real it was. The *Summa* constituted the path. Thomas could never have doubted the truth of the arguments which he sought to display by reason within it. The non-Christian philosopher is apt, therefore, to dismiss the *Summa* as an argument founded on preconceived premises, nor can it be doubted that there is some truth in the criticism. On the other hand, there was much that was reasonable in its philosophy,

[1] Cited from the *Quodlibeta* Ia 8 in M. C. D'Arcy's *The Mind and the Heart of Love*, 89 which has an interesting and impartial discussion on Thomas' theory of love.

nor does the criticism radically affect the relevance of Thomas' method and his conclusions. Certain aspects of his thought have naturally sunk into oblivion while others have become irrelevant. The astonishing thing is that so much of it retains its original interest and intellectual vitality. There were other critics who held that the marriage between faith and reason was unwarranted. Even in his own day there were those who charged Thomas with the propagation of semi-heretical ideas. Very soon after his death, the great scholastic thinkers of the fourteenth century, Duns Scotus and William of Occam, denied the validity of the reconciliation which he had affected between faith and reason and reverted to a dependence on faith. In many intellectual circles he suffered discredit as a representative of medieval obscurantism and reaction; no more absurd judgment has ever been promulgated.

For it is certain that no churchman ever had so great an influence over the future, with the possible exception of St. Augustine. His books were reprinted constantly in every century. Dante found him in Paradise. Richard Hooker was influenced by his arguments. For the Roman Catholics, he rightly became their most representative teacher. He was canonized less than fifty years after his death (in 1323) by one of the more secular-minded of the Popes, John XXII, made a doctor of the Church in 1567 and finally, in 1879, declared by Leo XIII the patron saint of all Roman Catholic schools and colleges. But this is certainly not the full extent of his influence. Some of the ablest writers of our day on theological and social questions, Gilson and Maritain in France in particular, have founded their philosophy on his. Much that is most relevant in modern Anglicanism depends finally on Aquinas' ideas.

Thomas' response to the crisis of his day was, therefore, no less relevant to the needs of our own day than those of the other figures whom we are considering. What he saw clearly was that only an integrated philosophy of existence could save the thought of his day from the dissolving factors which threatened it. The *Summa* was the answer, a tremendous exposition of the Christian faith, nor do its defects in any way impair the fact that it was probably the most positive book written by any Christian thinker since the *City of God*. He saw that the whole of man's life from the embryo to the grave, within the home, the State, the Church and the Empire, could only be properly apprehended within the framework of divine knowledge. It is towards the goodness of God, the vision of the Creator that man stretches out, the Christian gospel crowning, surpassing and embodying all else. In other words, Thomas provided man with a defined purpose based on a reasonable philosophy of life. Its fundamentals are undated, for more than any other medieval system of thought, its permanence was ensured by a silent, corpulent friar who thought on the things of God and wrought a majestic work. And when all is said and done, the scene which blinds the eye more than any other is the years' imprisonment in the castle of San Giovanni which preceded his life's work. Through suffering in mind, and perhaps in body, he had perfected love.

BOOKS FOR FURTHER READING

Summa Theologica, 22 vols., trans. 1912-25.

Summa Contra Gentiles, 5 vols., trans. 1924-29.

E. Gilson, *The Spirit of Medieval Philosophy*, trans. A. H. C. Downes, 1936.

E. Gilson, *The Philosophy of St. Thomas Aquinas*, trans. E. Bullough, 1937.

P. Rousselot, *The Intellectualism of Saint Thomas,* trans., 1935.

A. D. Sertillanges, *Saint Thomas d'Aquin*, 2 vols., Paris, 1910.

A. D. Sertillanges, *Foundations of Thomistic Philosophy*, trans. G. Anstruther, 1931.

M. Grabmann, *St. Thomas Aquinas*, 1929.

J. Maritain, *St. Thomas Aquinas*, trans. J. F. Scanlan, 1938.

G. K. Chesterton, *St. Thomas Aquinas*, 1933.

M. C. D'Arcy, *St. Thomas Aquinas*, 1930.

IV. John Calvin

IN THE sixteenth century, European thought was flung
into a metaphorical crucible from which a series of
differently shaped ideas were finally drawn. Yet they were
drawn inevitably from the same source, from the theology
of medieval Catholicism and the politico-social framework
of medieval Europe. It is as well to insist on this fact, if
only because so many men begin their history at the
Reformation, unmindful that medieval ideas continued to
influence the structure and thought of the following period
to a far greater degree than is ordinarily recognized. The
Reformation did not create a sudden break with the past.
It placed a new accent on ideas implicit in medieval life,
emphasizing the predestinarian views of Augustine, thrust-
ing out the influence of Aristotle and the Thomists by
reverting to an earlier conception of faith, opposing the
scriptures to reason and natural law and the laity to the
priesthood as the monastic and Franciscan movements had
both done at the start, and as constant sect movements had
done since the foundation of the Church. Why was
there a Reformation? Why did the English and the
Scandinavians, the Dutch, the Scots and the Swiss, to
mention the chief supporters of the Reformers' ideas,
revile the Pope of Rome and renounce doctrines which
had long been accepted by contemporary society? If such
a question is fundamental, it is no less difficult to answer.
The Reformation, like all great historical movements,
resulted from a combination of causes whose pressure was
never constant in any one period or in any one country.

68

In some countries it represented the approach of the national state to political maturity; Henry VIII of England and Gustavus Vasa of Sweden both wanted to cut the chain binding them to Rome without altering doctrine, to assert their political and spiritual independence. The same kind of motive influenced the Dutch in their war against the Spanish Catholics, the French Huguenot nobles against their King, and the German Protestant princes against the Catholic emperor. Nor was the economic motive lacking. The English middle and lower classes had long grumbled at the payment of taxes to Rome. It was no accident that Protestantism was particularly strong among the weavers of Lyons nor that it made an implicit appeal to the worthy Dutch burghers and the staid Genevese merchants. If it was untrue, as Max Weber had asserted, that the Protestant "Ethic" directly assisted the spread of capitalist economy, there is plenty of evidence to show that the Protestant state formed an excellent environment for financial and industrial advance.

The Reformation was still, however, primarily a religious movement. Politics and economics influenced its rise, contributed to its development and, on occasions, assumed a dominating force in its history, but the Reformation cannot be defined in these terms alone. It was a spiritual, theological and ethical reaction against the characteristics which were latent in later medieval Catholicism. It should never be forgotten that Protestantism was grounded on medieval belief and was influenced to an extent which its leaders never recognized by medieval ideas. But there were, none the less, certain developments which seemed to threaten what the Reformers held to be the inalienable characteristics of primitive Christianity. Unquestionably, Rome itself was the focal-point of their attacks, for it was Rome which in their view had led the betrayal. The successor of Peter had managed to combine spiritual and temporal power in a unique way in the hands of some of the earlier medieval popes, especially Hildebrand and Innocent III, but to an increasing extent later Popes had lost the spiritual seal of their office in temporal occupations, in utterly selfish family and communal feuds, in a feverish search for power and wealth which had seemed to contradict the principles of Christ as early as the age of Wycliff, and even before. If there was no doubt of the splendour of late Renaissance Rome, newly garnished with the lovely dome of Bramante's St. Peter's, or of the charm and diplomacy of the cardinals, no reader of the Gospels could feel entirely satisfied that this was the fulfilment of the Christian intention. But the headship could not of itself be dismissed merely because it was incompetent or materialistic. The Reformers reading their Bibles thought that it was unwarranted in scripture, and that there was much in catholic tradition grossly discordant with the teaching and life of the contemporary Church. It was the reaction of the spirit and of faith against the mundane compromise which the Church seemed to have made with secular ambition. They saw in the theology of their day the barren trivialities of a sterile scholastic system, in the higher officials of the Church an idle, self-interested priestcraft, in the ordinary clergy an apathetic, often ignorant official class living on the delusions which they fostered in the laity. There was no doubt that much of this was exaggerated and inaccurate. And yet in their criticisms of the contemporary religion they were suddenly flung back on to problems of a more profound nature, the inerrancy of the Roman institutions, the Petrine theory, the question of transubstantiation and the relationship between faith and works, between faith and reason. Suddenly through the shifting clouds, many of the Reformers saw that the whole world was in a melting pot, and they were forced back into the belief in predestination. In a world of dissolution it seemed to them historically true to say that world-development actually depended on a theory of time which admitted divine foreknowledge and selection. What they read had been read repeatedly in the Middle Ages, the Scriptures, the fathers, St. Augustine in particular, the decisions of the councils, the writings of Thomas and William of Occam, but they saw it all in a new light and in a new environment created by changing circumstances. Both Catholic and Reformer were in fact enveloped in a terrific crisis, the birth of modern western civilization out of the medieval embryo, which demanded a solution. The old standards had been so shaken that they could never be resurrected by Roman or Protestant. Everything, politics, economics, religion, combined to administer the death warrant to the later medieval view of society, even if it continued to remain a vital influence for centuries to come. Shakespeare's *King Lear*, like Rabelais' *Gargantua and Pantagruel*, were both symbolic of what was happening. Rabelais made the motto of his abbey of Thelema "Faites ce que voudras", furnishing his argument with a luxuriance and a sense of physical and intellectual well-being that has rarely been surpassed, but it would have been impossible to have embedded the abbey of Thelema even in Boccaccio's slightly feverish *Decameron Nights*. Shakespeare expressed in *King Lear* the feeling that the climax of the age was the scene of a great struggle between elemental forces in which men were as "flies to wanton boys". Each realized that there was a supreme crisis and each reacted differently. What was the religious reaction to the emergence of a new political, economic and religious order? Each man reinterpreted it according to his own notions, but three men were particularly representative in their reaction. John

Calvin, Ignatius Loyola and Richard Hooker each responded to the immense challenge of his own age in his own way, fundamentally for the future, each a profound contribution to religious truth, however different his message may appear to be.

At the end of the Lake the mountains, the silver-tipped Dent du Midi in particular, seem very close, but as the land grows less hilly the boat approaches Geneva where the two rivers Rhone and Arve, curiously different in colour, meet and flow into azure waters. There is a peculiar loveliness about Swiss lakes, a dryness of atmosphere, a translucence of sky and lake, which is conducive to thought, meditation and freedom.   The important city of Geneva was situated in the duchy of Savoy, but its government at the opening of the century was extraordinarily complex, the Bishop of Geneva, the local municipal government and the Duke of Savoy represented by a Vice-dom, all having some say in the governance of the city. The feuds which split the town do not concern us. They merely testify to the high feeling and independence of its citizens who soon took advantage of the rise of reformed opinion in Germany (under Martin Luther) and Switzerland to use it as a spur against both the Bishop and the Duke. The beginnings of the Reformation in Geneva were as closely linked with a combined series of motives as elsewhere, nor was the course of events very different. There was one exception—there was no one man informed enough or strong enough as a personality to lead and guide them. It was this difficulty which made Farel decide to ask John Calvin to help him in the reformation of the city in 1536. No more historic decision was made in the whole history of the Reformation.

Why was this twenty-seven year old Frenchman with his grave, unsmiling face selected? His early career did not give any particular promise of his future importance. His father, Gérard Cauvain, had risen to the position of a notary apostolic and Procurator Fiscal to the Bishop of Noyon where his second son, Jean, was born on July 10th, 1509. His father was a bourgeois but his ancestors before him had been watermen at Pont l'Evêque on the river Oise. It was therefore natural that Gérard hoped that his son might in due course rise to higher things. He managed to obtain the income of two benefices from the Chapter of Noyon and sent Jean to study theology, and later, law, at the universities of Paris, Orleans and Bourges. His legal and classical studies made an imprint on the boy's mind which was never removed; his theology was fashioned by judicial reasoning nor did it ever escape from the classical, humanistic background which had led him to edit Seneca's De Clementia. When or exactly how he questioned traditional Catholicism seems a little uncertain, but the rectorial address which he probably wrote for Nicholas Cop at the end of 1533 shows that he had advanced in his ideas since he penned the graceful De Clementia, published the previous year. The two influences which appear in this address go a long way to reveal the nature of the change: Erasmus' Greek Testament and Martin Luther's sermons. They suggest, what one might have expected from Calvin's subsequent writings, that his decision was intellectual rather than emotional. The original words of the Gospel afforded a great contrast with what Calvin (who, at his father's command had deserted the study of theology for that of law) knew of the teaching of the contemporary Church. There are no signs that Calvin had been particularly interested in religious ideas nor that his conversion to Protestantism had the dramatic "either–or" quality which we may associate with Augustine or Francis, Ignatius or John Wesley. Yet he could not escape discussing what was on everyone's lips in the society which he frequented nor could he have been ignorant of the fact that these French reformers were actually patronized by the French King's sister. The rest could be left safely to his intelligent, observant mind and to his reading. If the Greek Testament awakened in him a new knowledge of God, Luther's writings made him realize the importance of grace. It was this, diffused through the study of Augustine and Paul, which became more and more the centre-piece of his theological thought, as the later editions of his *Institutes* reveal; man stood sinful and impotent before the perfectly good, absolutely omnipotent God. And if God was omnipotent, He must also be omniscient, and man's ultimate fate must already be sealed before he plays his act upon the human stage. But all this as yet lay to some extent in the future.

Whatever the exact nature of the change of his faith, he left Paris, surrendered the benefices which his father (who had died in 1531) had acquired for him at Noyon, and in the winter of 1534 went to Basle. This Swiss city was the seat of a university of European renown and a gathering place for humanists and reformers from all over Europe. Learning was combined with religion to create Protestantism, nor could any other amalgam have proved so attractive to the scholarly mind of the young Frenchman. He had already arrived at the conclusions which lay at the root of his amazing system of thought, conduct and organization. It is true that certain aspects were developed and emphasized at a later date, but the foundations were secure and unalterable. They were contained in the *Institutes of the Christian Religion* which was prefaced by an open letter to King Francis I of France on behalf of the reformers. In the years that followed the original material was greatly expanded; by 1559 the six original chapters had increased to twenty-four. The book was published in 1536, the year in which Farel invited him to help in reforming Geneva.

The situation in the city by the lakeside was complex. In an effort to rid themselves of the authority of the Duke of Savoy and the Bishop, Pierre de la Baume, the Genevese had risen in revolt. To consolidate their success they had allied with the Bernese who had already adopted the Lutheran faith. Both these steps necessitated an equation of political independence with religious change. As sincere Protestants recognized, a change of faith did not mean a change of morals. The moral condition of both clergy and laity may have been no worse than that of other cities, but the peculiar conditions of Geneva, its compact nature, its traditional government had made the decline in morality the more marked. Farel, who has not perhaps received his full credit, initiated a series of reforms coupling doctrine with behaviour, which provoked considerable opposition. Realizing the immensity of the problem facing him, he persuaded Calvin, somewhat against his will, to stay to help him. "You", Farel told him, "make the excuse of your studies. But if you refuse to give yourself with us to this work of the Lord, God will curse you, for you are seeking yourself rather than Christ."

He remained in Geneva two years, suffered expulsion in 1538 and then, against his own inclinations, returned in 1541, dying twenty-three years later. These bare facts convey nothing of what took place in Geneva during this period, or the vast significance of Calvin's career in the world at large. Here was a comparatively young and even unknown man setting out to reform the life of a city, nor could anyone have accurately foreseen the force and influence of his personality. He is generally pictured as grim, austere and forbidding. Certainly there was a grimness which repels charm in his make-up; his treatment of the heterdox Servetus and other of his private enemies was unforgivable. His life had the austerity of the prophet whose sense of mission subordinates all else to the one abiding aim. There was a passionate enthusiasm never completely concealed behind the scholar who wrote so many books of commentaries or the humanist whose French is as liquid and as clear as a mountain stream. Calvin was not unfeeling. He was devoted to the wife whom he had married in Strasburg while his affection for Farel remained undimmed to the end, if clouded latterly by Farel's marriage to a girl some years younger than himself. The sincerity of his faith, the reality of prayer, the abiding love for God were unquestionable. The legislative nature of his theology may have given an awe-inspiring quality to his conception of God, which may be traced to his innate subordination of all to Him. His passionate enthusiasm made him over-confident, too certain of his decisions, too sure of his judgment and thus led him to approve of actions which, to say the least, lacked human charity. Yet his sincerity and honesty permeated all that he did. His organization was supreme, his efficiency and conscientiousness made Geneva into a model state for Calvinists. He never took a holiday, but rising early in the morning, worked without ceasing until illness and finally death brought his labours to an end. His virtues were not the virtues of a popular man and, for that reason, he had far more in common with Augustine than Francis. Furthermore, the intellectual nature of his personality, its prophetic ardour, concealed the native charm and sensitivity which lay beneath. Luther was emotional, so emotional that he could weep over a violet crushed by snow, whereas all that Calvin would permit himself was an occasional fit of depression, a few revealing words in an odd letter. His personality was steel-like, with the defects and advantages of steel, strong, fine, clear-cut, but often lacking in sympathy and love.

After the influence of environment and heredity, that of

theology was paramount in his development and in his approach to social and political questions. His works contain references to classical writers as well as to the medieval doctors, but his thought was far less affected by scholastic influences than that of Luther. His clear mind thrust aside the greater part of medieval doctrine and ritual as a tawdry superstructure only worthy of destruction. He went back to the New and Old Testament, of which he had an extraordinarily rich knowledge, and to St. Paul and St. Augustine. The challenge could only be met successfully by a theology which placed God and man in right relationship. It was here, he felt, that the Roman Catholics had so erred, for they had invented a series of devices intended to deflect or influence the divine will. There was thus the Pope's claim to be a successor of Peter, to embody his personality and to act as God's vicegerent, and of the clergy to act as mediators between God and man through the sacraments; the Mass itself was a clear perversion of the sacrament as it had been originally instituted. The theory of transubstantiation, the invocation of the Blessed Virgin Mary and the saints, the current practice of indulgences and pilgrimages, were all man-made devices intended to influence the action of God the creator. This seemed blasphemous to Calvin, particularly when man in his moral conduct seemed to make so few attempts to model his own life on the divine will. As he looked at the sun glinting on the snows of Mount Blanc far away, he must have felt that man might as well challenge the sublimity of a great mountain as seek to become good through his own will. This consciousness of man's sin, even more of human *hubris,* or arrogance, led Calvin, via St. Paul and St. Augustine, to throw himself completely before the grace of God. Man cannot save himself. His best actions cannot possibly influence the judgment of God. Everything must therefore depend on divine

decision, for God, and God alone, could save man. That
He would wish to do so goes without saying, for God is
implicitly gracious. If God was therefore independent of
human action, he must foreknow the future, nor does such
foreknowledge affect the apparent freedom of will which
man enjoys. God knows the answer, even if man does not.
Calvin was led to declare that the Church consisted of
those whom God had called, the "elect", by contrast with
the "reprobates" who were damned to hell. "We assert
that by an eternal and immutable counsel, God hath once
for all determined both whom he would admit to salvation
and whom he would admit to destruction. We confirm that
this counsel, as concerns the elect, is founded on his
gratuitous mercy totally irrespective of human merit; but
that to those whom he devotes to condemnation the gate of
life is closed by a just and irreprehensible judgment." The
statement was formidable, to some terrible, but it gave an
added strength to those who believed themselves to be the
elect, and was an exceptionally powerful weapon in the
fight against the old Church.

If the Church is ideally the circle of the elect, it must,
nevertheless, have some counterpart on earth. It is at this
stage that Calvin's thought slips from the realm of theology
almost imperceptibly into that of politics. For if Church
and State are in fact separate, they nevertheless constitute
"one society, distinct in function but inseparable in being".
The Church works inside the State which is equally divinely
ordered; but the State depends, in the last resort for ultimate law, on the statements of the Church. Both must
work together for the glory of God. Calvin may seem to
recall the medieval ideal but it is more probable that he was
influenced by the actual form of government, which Geneva
had long enjoyed. The Church deals with worship, doctrine
and the moral law. The State is therefore to enforce its

decisions, and to deal with questions affecting secular order and foreign policy. Yet they are completely inter-dependent.

This may so far appear to be a purely theoretical treatise. It is, however, the signal mark of the really great man that his thought must have a dynamic which forces it into practice. Evoked by a personal as well as a world crisis, it can never be confined within the four walls of the human mind or the pages of a book. Augustine's *City of God* had intense practical importance. Francis made the Christ real to thousands then and later. Thomas stamped the future of Roman theology with a practical as well as an intellectual character. Calvin was certain that the *Institutes* provided the foundation of Christian government, and made Geneva, as the Marxians later made Moscow, the centre of a great experiment. He was assisted by the peculiarly complicated nature of its past government which really left the muni-cipality in full control of both spiritual and temporal power after the bishop had been deposed in 1534. The city was also small enough in size to be the scene of a political and social experiment. Even if Calvin met with continuous opposition, he left his mark indelibly on its life. When he set about completing the work which he had begun with Farel in 1536, he continued to use the various city councils already in existence but the organization was extended, made systematic and all-embracing. The heads of families met together in the Great Council which elected the four Syndics and the Treasurer who were the city's leading officials. The Smaller Council acted as an executive com-mittee of the Greater Council. There was a Council of Sixty which formed a larger edition of the former and was called to deal with problems beyond the scope of the Smaller Council. The Church was governed in a corre-sponding way, according to the Ecclesiastical Ordinances

drawn up by Calvin. It was centred round the Ministry and
the Consistory. The Ministry formed the Venerable Company, met weekly in Congregation, examined those who left
themselves called to ordination, afterwards presenting those
whom they had passed to the Council for their approval,
studied the Scriptures, listened to sermons on doctrine and
acted as moral censors. The moral side was mainly the
special work of the Consistory, a council of six ministers and
twelve elders selected from the three Councils. The Consistory was, perhaps, the most representative institution in
the State since it realized Calvin's theocratic ideals. It acted
as a code of law for moral offences; the scope of its authority
was extraordinarily wide as any study of its Thursday
Meetings proves. Swearing, gambling, immorality, vice of
all descriptions were offences grouped side by side with
deviations from religious orthodoxy; a woman, for instance,
kneels upon her husband's grave and calls out "Requiescat
in pace" or a man sleeps in sermon time. Literally,
thousands of instances could be given where the crime
seemed trivial and the punishment ludicrous were it not
severe. Yet before we condemn, we should remember that
such discipline aimed to restore purity of life in a city
which had become accustomed to a low standard of morality.
Not all the offences were trivial nor all the punishments
unjust.

The Calvinist organization was perhaps the most significant of all Calvin's inventions and goes far to explain the
success which attended the Protestant movements that
adopted his ideas. The French Huguenot Church was, for
instance, placed in an immensely strong position *vis à vis* its
opponents simply because of its splendid organization
represented by its Consistory, Colloquy and Synod. But
Calvin created more than an organization; he made a
system. Geneva became a theocratic State par excellence,

where Church and State were truly facets of a single society, where the Bible was the foundation of law, and private and public morality were inseparable. Calvin built up an efficient ministry and sponsored the university and schools with such good effect that Protestants from all Europe fore-gathered at Geneva. Geneva was the centre of Protestant propaganda, the source of much wealth which went to subsidize Protestant movements in foreign countries and of enthusiastic missionaries. If Calvin was not naturally an attractive man, there was an element of leadership and of impassioned belief in the Gospel of God that made him revered, loved and respected. He was both the Marx and the Lenin of the Protestant Reformation, carrying its influence to Switzerland, Germany, Holland, Scotland and France.

John Calvin died on May 27th, 1564. His indomitable energy had carried him through constant illness, pleurisy calculus, gout, hærmorrhoidal ulcers, but he could not defeat the last enemy, pulmonary tuberculosis. After preaching a sermon in December, 1559, he coughed blood, but he laboured on; a new edition of the *Institutes, Commentaries* on the Minor Prophets, the Pentateuch, Jeremiah, Lamentation and Joshua. The fever gave, as it so often does, an added urgency to his writing. On Easter Day, 1564, he received the Communion for the last time, in the cathedral of St. Pierre. A few weeks later he made his will, a document which proves completely that he had never used his office to enrich himself. On the Friday before Whitsun he bade the Venerable Company farewell. Eight days later he died. It is exceptionally difficult to record a verdict, for if he was one of the best hated men in contemporary society, he was also one of the most revered; des Gallars, writing in 1570, recorded a common feeling: "When I look back upon his frankness and integrity, his affectionate benevolence

D

towards me and the familiar intimacy, which I enjoyed for
sixteen years, I cannot but grieve for my separation from
such a friend or, I would say, such a father. What labours,
watchings and anxieties did he endure! With what wisdom
and perspicacity did he foresee all dangers and how skilfully
did he go out to meet them! No words of mine can declare
the fidelity and prudence with which he gave counsel, the
kindness with which he received all who came to him, the
clearness and promptitude with which he replied to those
who asked for his opinion on the most important questions,
and the ability with which he disentangled the difficulties
and problems which were laid before him. Nor can I
express the gentleness with which he would console the
afflicted and raise the fallen and distressed, or his courage
and moderation in prosperity." This was no mere eulogy
nor can the reader of his sermons or commentaries as well
as his more private letters readily forget the intensity of the
faith and love which sustained him throughout his career.

Calvinism was indeed one answer to the crisis of the
Reformation. Confronted by religious and social anarchy
which might follow the potential dissolution of Catholicism,
Calvin found order and expectation in the Christian gospel.
He discarded past tradition too generously and framed a new
gospel based on his own interpretations of what the early
Church had been like. That this was by the standards of
history quite unrecognizable in the highly civilized city
State of Geneva is beside the point. He saw that what the
world needed was a new understanding of the transcendence
of God, a purer conception of the nature of God, and of the
relationship existing between God and his creature, man.
Man was completely the slave of God, so much so that he
could not achieve salvation of his own accord. His view of
the Sacraments was equally clear-cut; he discarded traditional belief and yet still—with certain modifications into

which there is no time to go—regarded them as an effective means of grace and remembrance. It was unfortunate that he should have insisted on predestination, more particularly as his interpretation of this doctrine suggested a measure of cruelty in the Creator in no way compatible with Calvin's own interpretation of divine personality. But the mind of Calvin was so logical, so taut, that he could not conceive of a God who was not absolute in knowledge and in selection. If Calvin had been asked, if you are predestined to salvation or to damnation, why not engage in what you want to do irrespective of consequences, he would have answered that predestination did not work that way, that the search for virtue was a sign of divine election, whether on the part of the individual or the community. But theologically, Calvin was principally important because of the way in which theology became so essentially practical in the model Church-State of Geneva.

Calvinism revitalized Christianity, enriching the great story of Puritanism in every country and leading, despite the aristocratic nature of Calvin's own rule in Geneva, to the formation of democracy in Church and State. Its defects of idea and practice are obvious. Its intolerance and self-complacency were ugly. Its narrowness and lack of sympathy, its pursuit of the economic virtues, its demolition of tradition, its tendency to under-estimate the part of the sacraments, to emphasize fear rather than joy, have all been censured by thinking Christians, but this is to judge a great movement by detail. Whether one deplores the rise of Calvinism or not, John Calvin responded to the challenge of his age with an intellectual clarity, and a measure of faith rarely matched in the sixteenth century. He believed that the Roman Church could not supply primal or Christian order. He realized the intrinsic weaknesses of Lutheranism and Zwinglianism. As in a flash, he wrote the *Institutes* which supplied the world with what he believed to be a model Christian republic. Looking back on the past twenty-eight years of his life, there was much that he would have changed, much that he had said in anger or in haste, but there was a sincerity, a God-formed decision as strong as that which influenced Augustine, Francis or Aquinas. And behind that there was a sense of spiritual reality which was far too often concealed in the "law and the prophets"; "if it is true", he wrote of the Sacrament of the Eucharist, "that the visible sign is offered to us to attest the granting of the invisible reality, then, on receiving the symbol of the body, we may be confident that the body itself is no less given to us . . ." The splendour of his faith was as a great mountain which awes and yet attracts the climber, but which it is given to few to climb.

Books for Further Reading

Calvin, *Institutes of the Christian Religion.*

Hugh Thompson Kerr, *A compend of the Institutes of the Christian Religion,* 1945.

Mitchell Hunter, *The Teaching of Calvin,* 1920.

B. Warfield, *Calvin and Calvinism,* 1931.

R. N. Carew Hunt, *Calvin,* 1933.

J. McKinnon, *Calvin and the Reformation,* 1936.

E. Doumergue, *Jean Calvin,* 7 vols., 1899-1927.

Imbart de la Tour, *Calvin et L'Institution Chretienne,* 1935.

V. St. Ignatius Loyola

THERE IS a great contrast between the fresh countryside around the smooth-flowing Oise which formed the background to Calvin's forebears and that where Ignatius Loyola, the young nobleman of Guipuzcoa, spent his youth. Superficially the two men were strikingly different in character. Yet, taking the differences into account, it may be that the contrast has been over-emphasized. Both the highly cultured, widely read French scholar and the under-educated but shrewd Spaniard were concerned with a similar task, the rehabilitation of the Church in face of the crisis which threatened it. They would certainly have disagreed as to the constitution of the Church and as to the nature of the crisis, but the methods they adopted were not so far apart. Calvin invented a supremely good organization which aimed at the conversion of secular life to religion. Loyola founded a society which represented the Church militant, based on rules but marked by no special uniform. Both Calvinism and Jesuitry lived in the world and were permeated by the notion that obedience to the Church was essential to success. Nor was it an accident that both the Calvinist and the Jesuit had so emphatic a realization of what the Church meant that they evoked the suspicions of autocratic authority and so suffered distrust. One further idea brings Loyola and Calvin close together, their awareness of sin and the saving love of God. Both Calvin and Loyola realized man's smallness before God, even if the one preferred faith as contrasted with works as the resultant and necessary response, and both were threaded with *amor Dei*

85

which ran through their souls and stimulated all their action.

The contrast may appear forced. It is certainly unusual. Nevertheless, both were drawn by the challenge of their age to offer an answer which was rooted in the love of God. If Calvinism confronted the disintegration of society with a theology and an organization that was above all logical and clear-cut, Loyola invested Catholicism with a new conception of the Church's task. Perhaps this phrase is too definite. Loyola did not think out anew the problem of the Church. He accepted current Catholic notions but he swept away many past prejudices and invented an original method of bringing home to men and women the meaning of the Church. What he did was fresh, original, tremendous. It has the sweep of a great symphony, the impression of a new style of art, even, on occasion, as in the seventeenth century model mission of Paraguay,[1] that of a new social structure. It was impounded confidently on the Church of the medieval world, to a more marked degree than the Genevan experiment, but it was, nevertheless, a new response to the contemporary crisis.

The Catholic world of the early sixteenth century had been compelled, with some reluctance in high places, to examine the abuses which the reformers outlined with some virulence. It had been long recognized that the Church was in need of reform, that the standard of education was low, that there was a great deal too much superstition and too little theology, that there were too many prelates without vocation, too many priests without responsibility, too many monks with nothing to do. Such things had been emphasized at the great Council of Constance, nor had the situation in any way improved since that assembly had dispersed in

[1] R. B. Cunninghame Graham's *A Vanished Arcadia*, 1901, affords an interesting introduction. Cf. P. Hernandez, *Misiones del Paraguay*, 2 vols. 1913.

1418. Chastened by this knowledge, the more responsible leaders of the Church initiated a series of reforms which at last led to a transformation of the Vatican itself. New orders were established, older orders were reformed, greater attention was paid to devotion and learning while the great Council of Trent which first met in 1545 and ended its discussions, after manifold interruptions in 1563, defined the faith of the Church more effectively than had ever been done before. It also published a series of decrees instituting reforms in the life of the Church. Finally, it made it perfectly clear that no possible compromise could be reached with Protestantism. Such decrees had comparatively little immediate effect in the Catholic world, for the sixteenth century was an active age, in general, more influenced by example than intellectual argument. It appreciated nothing better than a good discussion but it was more affected by the activity of its citizens than the doctrine of its thinkers. It preferred Drake to Ascham, Luther to Melancthon, Calvin to Beza and Loyola to Dr. Eck. It was no accident that a leading part in the proceedings of the Council of Trent was played by a dark-haired Spaniard, Diego Laynez, of the Society of Jesus. He and his colleagues had found themselves poorly welcomed, and badly housed, but no man more strikingly influenced the decisions reached by the assembled fathers. And this was particularly appropriate, for the society which he represented was the most active force in promoting the Counter-Reformation and formed, as it were, the spearhead of modern Catholicism.

It is often said that the founder of the Jesuits was a medievalist who drew his ideas from the life of Christ written by Ludolph of Saxony and his inspiration from the chivalric orders of the Middle Ages. He was, as were Calvin, Luther and Hooker, influenced by medieval example, but he was no more medieval than the Counter-Reformation Church of which he was so illustrious a representative. His early life affords an interesting comparison and contrast with that of the other Christian leaders whom we have so far examined. He was born about 1491 and served in the army, taking a part in the insignificant siege of Pampluna where on a spring day, a cannon ball shattered his leg. This formed the initial phase in the change, like Augustine's departure to Milan or Francis' first illness, for there is nothing of remote importance in the little evidence of his boyhood. He was already well advanced in youth, probably thirty, an ordinary, blustering soldier of noble birth, with a great and vain desire to win renown. During his convalescence, inability to obtain the chivalric romances which formed the staple reading of the Spanish upper classes, compelled him to read about Christ and the saints. This set up a train of imagination and meditation which formed a prelude to an intense spiritual experience, a complete reorientation of the whole of his life. He vowed to visit Jerusalem and began to copy excerpts from the holy books which he now read, with incredible patience "putting the words of Christ in red ink and those of our Lady in blue". His wound cured, he made his way to the sanctuary of Montserrat where, on March 24th, 1522, he spent the night in vigil before the altar of the Blessed Virgin. He retired to a cave outside Manresa and was rewarded with a vision of the Holy Trinity. A vision has only a contemporary and individual experience. It is incapable of being transferred to a detached observer except through the mark which it makes on the recipient. It branded Loyola for life; the reality of the vision appears through the Society of Jesus. His life had become ascetic, cruelly austere, and introspective; "there (at the cave of Manresa)", says the modern historian of the order, "he went through the dread mysterious Dark Night of the Soul . . . and there too he was caught up into Paradise and heard secret words which it is not granted to man to utter."[1] This "Dark Night of the Soul", so essentially a mystical experience, forms the ineradicable prelude to fulfilled experience. If its stress and intensity differs according to the temperament and nature of the individual, it appears always as the dawn of re-invigorated, re-integrated life. The intense struggles of Augustine in the garden at Milan, the impassioned agony of Francis as he gradually discarded all the conventions of the paternal house, the escape which Thomas made from the feudal life of Aquino, the slow piercing of accepted truth by Calvin, were all aspects of the same thing, but in Loyola there was a queer brightness, a burning flame which threatened to turn the former soldier into a mere ascetic. But he emerged from this struggle intensely stronger, aware that austerity of life was not in itself the answer to the supreme crisis of his age; "Seeing the fruit reaped from helping other souls, he ceased from this time from the extreme severities which he had been wont to practise, and also he began to cut his nails and his hair."

The more immediate result was the *Spiritual Exercises*. Unless it is realized that this embodies the spiritual struggles of a singularly sensitive personality who at an age when most men know what the future pattern of their lives is to be was only slowly realizing his vocation, its importance will be misunderstood. It reveals first of all how real the spiritual order had become to him. He saw that Christ was the King, that the monarchical conception of society which was familiar to all sixteenth-century Europeans was only understandable in the light of the more splendid truth that all the trappings of kingship, of military rule, had been spiritualized. Christ was a general going forth to conquer,

[1] J. Brodrick, *The Origin of the Jesuits*, 16.

but conquest is impossible without fighting, without self-mastery. The mental conflict which had moulded his life at Manresa and Barcelona became dramatized in a world battle for salvation, which could only be achieved through the choice of a path leading onwards through the battle towards God. There was, perhaps, nothing new in the argument, save its additional ardour and vitality. The imagery was concrete, the reality was spiritual. The reader imagined the *via Crucis,* fastened his whole thoughts on the preparation which leads finally to the consummation in the Passion. The *Spiritual Exercises* were far more than devotional literature; they provided a course of training for infinite existence, the spiritual reality forming the foundation for action.

It is this intransigent activity that makes them so important, for they at once remove Loyola and the Christians who read them out of the arena of pious meditation into that of practical politics. Christ's life was resurgent, active, an essay in faith reflected through works. So, too, with the follower of Loyola and with Loyola himself. Like Calvin, and other great leaders, there are times when the general's efficiency and impassioned enthusiasm seem to sacrifice charity to the self-assumed service of God, but in moments of quiet reflection, of letter-writing,[1] the ardour of love makes itself felt as the real stimulus to life. From Spain he went to Rome and thence he walked to Venice where he obtained a passage on a ship which brought him to Cyprus and led him at last to Jerusalem. On his return, increasingly fortified by experience, he resumed his broken education. Nothing is more humiliating than to begin learning at

[1] The number of letters, written by the first Generals, which survive provide an excellent illustration of their unstinted industry. Over six thousand of Ignatius' letters exist, while Laynez despatched some 2,379 letters during his sixteen months' stay at Trent. (*Progress of Jesuits,* 110.) Brodrick also mentions that the correspondence of the famous Peter Canisius who laboured in Germany with such great success "fills eight large octavo volumes of 7,550 pages". (*op. cit.,* 149 n.)

thirty-one beside those whose mental receptivity is so much greater than one's own. Loyola found the divine lesson in humiliation. He drew followers and made enemies, especially among the Spanish clergy who looked askance at his curious way of doing things and at the growth of his band of disciples. Banned from teaching at the University of Alcala, he made his way with three companions to the University of Salamanca, only to find himself in prison again in less than a fortnight. Perhaps, he thought, France would view his mission more favourably. "By the grace and goodness of God, Our Lord, in favourable weather and safe and sound, I arrived in this city of Paris on February 2nd, resolved to study there until such time as the Lord shall otherwise ordain."

If Loyola met Calvin it must have been at the College Montaigu whither he went before he attended the more humane College of Sainte-Barbe. It seems unlikely, for the intelligent, if comparatively ignorant, Spaniard approaching middle age would have had little in common with the young classical scholar; his patience was rewarded with a master's degree in 1534. It was in Paris that he found six men of similar enthusiasm, the Frenchman, Pierre Favre, Diego Laynez, Alfonso Salmeron, Nicholas "Bobadilla", Simon Rodriguez and Francis Xavier, a Spanish Basque like himself of singularly enchanting disposition, and it was here on the Feast of the Assumption, 1534, at a Mass celebrated by Favre, as yet the only priest among them, that they made a vow to live a life of poverty and chastity and to go to Jerusalem to convert the heathen.

The next five years formed a period of preparation. Except for the *Spiritual Exercises,* the advance to this decision has revealed nothing very unique, excepting Loyola's unceasing energy and devotion. The years which followed formed no exception to this. In many ways they betray a

narrowness of vision and a traditional conception of duty.
His followers did not think in terms of a great world-wide
task but, like some medieval monks, of themselves as
missionaries sent to secure the return of the Holy Land from
the Turks to the Christian faith. They lived lives of service
and study; "to tend the patients," so Rodriguez describes
their work at two Venetian hospitals, "make the beds,
sweep the floors, scrub the dirt, wash the pots, dig the
graves, carry the coffins, read the services (all, except
Salmeron who was as yet too young, were now ordained to
the priesthood) and bury the dead." They were not even
a religious order and they were still distrusted by the local
clergy of the districts where they worked. But Ignatius'
conception of his task was slowly widening, coming to
maturity as he realized that the Turkish peril made the
conversion of Palestine a virtual impossibility. He became
increasingly aware that the crisis facing the Church was
frontal and European rather than Turkish, that Protestantism
constituted a greater enemy than infidelity. He had already
placed himself and Xavier at the disposal of the Pope before
he decided to form a rule which was, after a good deal of
opposition from Cardinal Guidiccioni, embodied in the bull
Regimini militantis Ecclesiae in 1540.

The bull was a landmark in the history of the Church.
It established a religious society which constituted nothing
less than a living embodiment of the Church militant here
on earth. Loyal above all to the vicar of Christ, they were
next in duty bound to give complete and unswerving obedience to the General of the order, an office which Loyola
accepted with some reluctance, "Let us", runs the appropriate passage in the Constitutions, "with the utmost pains
strain every nerve of our strength to exhibit this virtue of
obedience, firstly to the Highest Pontiff, then to the
Superiors of the Society . . . and let each one persuade

himsēlf that they that live under obedience ought to allow themselves to be borne and ruled by divine providence working through their Superiors exactly as if they were a corpse which suffers itself to be borne and handled in any way whatsoever; or just as an old man's stick which serves him who holds it in his hand wherever and for whatever purpose he wish to use it . . ." The discipline was strict, the obedience automatic because the task was so supremely important, no less than the redemption of the world for the Catholic faith. Ignatius was perfectly certain that all other forms of Christianity were insidious inrushes of the Devil, only made the more attractive by their apparent freedom. A successful soldier fights with undeviating obedience to his superior officer, willing to suffer all the wounds and bitterness of the campaign, asking only to fulfil his duty, "for no reward save that of knowing Thee". If the Franciscan was the tumbler of the Lord, the Jesuit was the mercenary of God, dispensed from the duty of singing the monastic hours in choir[1] or from the duty of wearing the monastic garb, graded according to his spiritual efficiency and true vocation. It is sometimes urged that the Jesuit lost his individuality in identifying himself with the institution. There is no answer to this except in the feeling of dependence on God (felt by Calvin as much as by Loyola) which the Jesuit believed was exercised through the Pope and his representative. "Altogether I must not desire to belong to myself, but to my Creator and His representative. I must let myself be led and moved as a lump of wax lets itself be kneaded, must order myself as a dead man without will or judgment." The perils confronting Catholic civilization could only be overcome by an unexampled effort of will; "like a mighty army moves the Church of God" under the command of the

[1] This was a source of constant discord with different popes in the early history of the order.

Jesuit general against the foe. The only perturbing point about such a belief was the fact, somewhat pleasing to the cynical mind, that the foe was invested with exactly the same notion. But this is to temper a grave historical fact with flippancy. The Jesuits were the fifth-column of the Vatican, an international society, learned, and enthusiastic, working for the salvation of souls through teaching and good works. It would be wrong to leave the significance of Ignatius' society here. The General was no more ignorant of the world and its wiles than Booth of the Salvation Army three hundred years later. He had a more realistic view of human nature than John Calvin and did not need to under-pin his religion with the idea of predestination. Calvin presented Geneva with a dramatic challenge; the world which can only be redeemed through the unmerited grace of God must be bent to the divine will through the will of the Church. Loyola possessed no consistory but he was equally clear that the world must be redeemed by the Church. Yet he saw that if this was to be attained the Church must woo rather than force the world to faith. Calvin emphasized duty, Loyola courtship. The Calvinist thought of man as the erring bridegroom who must be reminded of the absolute ethic of the society he had scorned. The Jesuit regarded man as the possible betrothed of the Lord; even a broken engagement could be remedied with good will. "Loyola", says a dispassionate modern observer, "came to the conclusion that the Church must fully utilize the existing organs of education, of discipline, even of entertainment; it must turn pomp and worldliness themselves to its own uses. On these matters, Loyola was far more revolutionary than Calvin and Luther; for whereas they recoiled from the New World that had opened before them, Loyola both figuratively and actually sought to embrace it."[1]

[1] Lewis Mumford, *The Condition of Man*, 1944, 224.

Such was something of the meaning of the bull of 1540. Loyola lived another sixteen years, directing the work of his followers with forethought and interest. His letters, which were sent to every corner of the world, reveal the multifarious duties, which now engaged his time. He never lost his sense of balance, his moderation, nor is there perhaps a more striking contrast than that between the ecstatic Francis with his inability to discipline his thoughts about such matters as the constitution of the friars and the equally saintly Basque with his command over detail and his quiet efficiency. He was not always so quiet—there were moments when he blazed out in anger at the stupidity or disobedience of one of the fathers. Yet the task called for unceasing labour, even though the eyes continued to shine brightly in the ageing face. The rapid expansion of the order was a satisfying memorial to the long toil, the vigilant watch for spiritual reality; by 1556 there were some thousand Jesuits grouped together in twelve provinces. Wherever the Counter-Reformation was making headway against Protestantism or scepticism, or wherever Christianity was being preached against the heathen, the Jesuit Fathers were well to the forefront. In time to come, some evil was perpetrated in the name of good, the moral standard was sometimes lowered to gain an immediate victory, wealth was garnered with trade and stored to build lovely baroque or churrigueresque churches, or on occasions to interfere by intrigue in politics or to short-cut dangerous, progressive thought. If Pascal condemned the Jesuits with insufficient evidence in the *Provincial Letters,* the world cannot forget moments of discredit in their past history. Yet as Ignatius last turned the pages of the Missal in 1556, he could be sure that he had raised a splendid monument, nor could he take responsibility for future wrongs. His vision was limited, as is that of all men, but he had followed it with unstinting devotion. "Once risen from the state and free from the affection of mortal sin", he had written in the *Spiritual Exercises,* "we may then speak of that filial fear which is truly worthy of God, and which gives and preserves the union of pure love." It was that "filial fear" which had led to the creation of the Society of Jesus.

It is now possible to estimate with greater accuracy the significance of Loyola's response to the challenge of his times. Yet the Jesuits still live under a stigma which was affixed to their society earlier in history. If they were accused in the past of casuistical morality and of political intrigue designed to favour their order and the Papacy against national sovereigns, which led ultimately to their dissolution in 1773, since their reconstitution in 1814 they have continued to evoke hostility from all quarters, not excluding some from the other Roman orders. While it is true that their records will not stand up to a close investigation,[1] perhaps to no less a degree than any other important institution, the reason for this continued hostility is contained primarily in the essential nature of Loyola's own response. He saw that the real challenge to the contemporary church lay in the deviation of loyalty from the Pope to national sovereigns or Protestant leaders. The Pope could no longer count, even in Roman Catholic countries, on the unqualified devotion and loyalty of his subjects, for if they had not imbibed heresy they were certainly, clergy and laity alike, bound to recognize and obey the law of the State rather than the natural law of the Church. Loyola hoped that the other objects of the society might prevent the danger from coming to a climax, but he certainly realized that the trend of development in all European states was alien to the universal and international authority

[1] Yet critics of the Jesuits would be astounded at the display of devotion, courage and piety which printed letters and documents reveal.

of the Roman Catholic Church. This is reflected in the constant opposition which the Jesuits experienced from the Bishop and the Theology Faculty of the University of Paris. ''The Pope'', said Bishop Eustache du Bellay, ''has no power to approve an order in this country, but only in his own States.'' It was no accident that King Philip II of Spain, the most catholic of contemporary monarchs in the sixteenth century, brought the Spanish Church as completely as possible under his control nor that France in the seventeenth century witnessed the rise of anti-papal forces which led to a breach with Rome. In Germany, eighteenth-century Febronianism, which tried to make the Pope into a constitutional monarch, constituted a parallel to French Gallicanism. Whatever the artifice employed, except for political reasons arising out of an internal political situation, Catholic States ought to evade their responsibility to Petrine headship if matters came to a climax. The answer to such a state of affairs must lie in the creation of an order of men whose absolute duty and obedience was, under their general, to the Pope. Laynez, who became the second general of the order, was the natural advocate of papal claims at the great sixteenth-century Council of Trent, such a position becoming indeed representative. The Society of Jesuits was bound first of all in loyalty to the Pope, a loyalty which by its very nature could free them from all other obligations. In theory, and to some extent in practice too, they cut loose from all the obligations by which every other citizen of the State was bound, simply because such obligations were only valid in so far as they might be identified with the principles of divine natural law. Thus, while it is correct to state that Jesuit moral theology differed from that of the Dominicans and some other Catholic orders, the difference was concerned less with the lowering of standards than with the greater emphasis on the subordination of the individual to the claims of his Church. If the Jesuit was willing to compromise with the world, it was only that he might emphasize the greater loyalty to God's Church represented through God's vicegerent, the Pope. It is perfectly clear that such an attitude aroused intense suspicion among the nationally minded peoples of Europe. When, at a later date, it tended to become wedded to political and intellectual reaction, such disgust knew no bounds, but the animus arose, less from these less pleasant characteristics, than from the close association between the Order and the Pope, which has existed since Paul III issued the bull, *Regimini Militantis Ecclesiae,* until now, "Always", reads the *Spiritual Exercises,* "to be ready to obey with mind and heart, setting aside all judgment of one's own, the true spouse of Jesus Christ, our holy mother, our infallible and orthodox mistress, the Catholic Church, whose authority is exercised over us by the hierarchy." The very nature of the Jesuit constitution, the personality of Ignatius, all led to the sounding of a trumpet note which was far more the assertion of a great challenge than that offered by any other Catholic body of his time. It was because Loyola made so much of the international nature of Catholicism and of the unilateral loyalty that it entailed that the society both aroused suspicion and fulfilled his trust.

This is, of course, a later interpretation of Loyola's methods. He did not anticipate that the challenge of his own age could be met profitably by a renewal of conflict. The oneness of the allegiance and the international nature of the society formed, as it were, the foundation and the reserve which could be used, if circumstances provoked the occasion, to defeat the enemy. Both Loyola and his followers realized only too well that the world of the sixteenth century could not be overcome by a sudden, catastrophic challenge. Jesuit theology, as its opponents understood, reacted more sympathetically towards the sinner than any other system, even if ultimately the Jesuit maintained as high a standard of morality as other Christian thinkers. In appearance at least the Jesuit mingled more with the world than the monk, but such apparent compromise was in fact only part of the strategy by which he might assist in the world's redemption. There was, however, a difference between Calvinism and Jesuitry since where Calvinism emphasized the obligations of the Christian, obligations ultimate in themselves since they did not affect salvation, the Jesuit made much more of the rewards which Christian action would ensure and of the ultimate attraction of the Christian life.

It was, therefore, inevitable that the Jesuits should be, above all, teachers and missionaries, for their order was a living and militant expression of the Collegium de Propaganda Fide, which Pope Gregory XV founded in 1622. "I promise", said the Fourth Vow, "special obedience to the Pope regarding the missions." Loyola had intended originally that his order should cater principally for his own recruits. In 1542, the famous college was started at Coimbra which was soon sending missionaries to far quarters of the earth. Within the next four years, hostels were started at the university towns of Italy and Spain, at Padua, Valencia, Alcala, Salamanca, but with the idea of catering for the Jesuit novices rather than for the general public. The beginning of a new order of affairs dates from the foundation of the University of Gandia by that saintly aristocrat, Francis Borgia, Duke of Gandia, who did so much to redeem a name blackened by the reputation of its past members. Gandia's gift meant that henceforth the Jesuits were to take their place in the university world as lecturers and teachers and to open schools and colleges for the laity as well as for their brethren. A further important step occurred when Gandia's munificence enabled Loyola to found the famous Gregorian University of Rome, the Collegio Romano; the first ordinary school, the College of Billom, started its life in July, 1556. From this time onward they never looked back, nor did any one ever dispute the excellence of the Jesuit education. What challenge there was arose, indeed, from the fact of its excellence. They stimulated interest by original methods, spurred on competition by the use of marks, and proved particularly inventive in their treatment of mathematics and astronomy. But they were clear as to their final object, the conversion of the soul to the glory of God. Whether the school was a mission school in some Chinese village or the famous College de Louis le Grand, object and method were familiar, the injection of the pupil with the Jesuit view of life, in full accordance with their original aims as defined in the bull of 1540.

One other characteristic of Jesuit education requires mention. Accepting the social and governmental structure of society as they found it, they preferred to conquer rather than change the social structure. They were therefore especially interested in the education of the future governors of the State and of members of the ruling classes. They became tutors in royal households, often retaining their influence, especially with the Hapsburg family of Austria, long after their pupils had grown up, for the tutor was often replaced by the confessor; a vigorous personality could influence politics from the confessional surer than the foreign secretary could from a cabinet meeting. The history of the Bourbons of Spain could, indeed, be written from the standpoint of the confessional, even the nineteenth-century Isabella II allowing herself to be influenced unduly by her confessor, Father Claret.

Education and missionary work form two aspects of a single unity, for what is education if it is not missionary work in the broader sense? From the very start the General sent his missionaries to labour in India and China while others went at a later date to South America, Abyssinia and Quebec. There are few more thrilling stories than the saintly devotion displayed by many of the Jesuit missionaries, none more thrilling or fascinating than the story of Saint Francis Xavier, one of Loyola's original followers, whose enthusiasm and courage transcended every obstacle. Their ventures were everywhere characterized by the same supreme impassioned enthusiasm for the Christian message and the same undivided loyalty. They did not court martyrdom, even if many suffered it, but sought to win souls by interest and sympathy, stimulated by the same urge that sent them as missionaries to Elizabeth's England or Hapsburg Bohemia. Father Matteo Ricci adopted native costume, and captured the interest of the Chinese Emperor by his knowledge of science. The moderatism of their teaching, their attempt to reconcile their environment to their message, made them outstandingly successful as missionaries.

The limitations of the Society of Jesus were probably inseparable from the nature of the rule, the suppression of the individual in the name of the community, their primary loyalty to the pontiff and the general, the despotic nature of their government, their concern with a final object which led them at periods of their history to abuse the means, but these defects neither affect the significance of Loyola's work nor the response which he had made to the challenge of his time. It may well be that more than any single man or woman he contributed to the reformation of the Catholic Church and the reinfusion of vigour which enabled her to face the future with delimited numbers but unchastened enthusiasm. And this was because for all his efficiency and moderation, Loyola always had his mind and soul focused on the greater loyalty which lies beyond the world. "We must", he told Sister Teresa Rejadilla, "lift ourselves up in true faith and hope in the Lord." This was the ultimate secret of Loyola's success.

Books for Further Reading

St. Ignatius Loyola, *The Spiritual Exercises*, ed. W. H. Longridge, 1930.

H. D. Sedgwick, *St. Ignatius Loyola*, 1923.

Paul van Dyke, *St. Ignatius Loyola*, 1926.

J. Brodrick, *The Origin of the Jesuits*, 1940.

J. Brodrick, *The Progress of the Jesuits*, 1946.

VI. Richard Hooker

THE REFORMATION was more than a religious upheaval; it was a revolution. Yet much that was done by the reformers had occurred also in past ages. Mobs had attacked churches and burnt down abbeys; noble lords had enriched themselves with ecclesiastical property and sold the lead from the roofs of churches. Kings had stripped alien churchmen of their privileges and had defied the Pope with impunity. Even doctrine had been challenged, by the Hussites in Bohemia or the Lollards in England for instance, without a reformation occurring. Fundamentally, however much the sources of the Reformation might lie in the medieval past, what was changing was the attitude of mind towards religious questions. If men and women still thought within the medieval framework of society, the general tendency of the age was towards a new, transformed ethic of society at work within a world that was broadening its borders in every possible way. The response to this particular crisis differed greatly from individual to individual. As we have seen, Calvin sought to return to a more primitive state interpreted, however, through the eyes of his own age. The city state of Geneva and the Presbyterian Church were the result, in effect certainly cutting astride a whole stream of development and omitting factors that were closely inter-related to the organic evolution of society. The thread of tradition became a string from which those who wished might, at least with intellectual impunity, break loose if they felt so inclined. However powerful its organization, Calvinism did in fact release the individual from his subservience to a supernatural authority embodied in a divinely ordained Church. This had been far from Calvin's intention, but that was how his ideas worked out in practice, so that the Dutch Reformed Church broke into two segments, while the Scottish Presbyterians were affected by repeated schisms, and American Calvinism became the foster-father of the greater number of the 256 sects[1] and churches now to be found in the United States. On the other hand, in the hands of Loyola the thread of tradition became a rope. If again Loyola was in fact far more of a radical and far less of a conservative than Calvin, Loyola's foundation, the Society of Jesus, became in the course of time the embodiment of many of the more reactionary and authoritarian elements in Roman Catholic theology and politics. Where Calvinism suffered from under-emphasis, Jesuitry was impeded by its over-emphasis on the traditions of the past.

Where did moderation lie? Where was there a response which seemed to combine what was best in the past with what was most expedient and just in the present and provided for further developments in the future? If there is an answer to this question, it is undoubtedly to be found above all in the works of a country parson, Richard Hooker. Hooker's response to the crisis of the revolution was that which, in the opinion of the present writer, stands most satisfactorily against the background of past and future history and is most in line with past historical development. The innate suitability of Hooker's answer lies in the very fact that he was able to refer to the past without impeding the future.

The history of the English Reformation reflects the crisis of the Reformation in miniature. Most people are acquainted with the rough outline. The second of the Tudor kings, a man of culture, and masterly ingenuity,

[1] W. L. Sperry, *Religion in America*, 1945, 73.

Henry VIII by name, was beset by matrimonial troubles resulting from political considerations and personal affections or, more bluntly, lusts, for if Henry was a great King and an able politician, no one can deny that he was lacking in spiritual and moral perceptions. However, be that as it may, this finely-featured monarch discovered that the Pope was unwilling to dissolve his marriage with his Spanish wife, Catherine of Aragon. The slow delay, the tortuous diplomacy, the continual galloping of horses bearing the royal messengers and the whispered conversations of red-robed cardinals, the greed of high-born and arrogant nobles who hated the subtle, scheming Wolsey, formed the background to the developing scene. At last the King was convinced that he must solve the problem by by-passing the Pope. The Archbishop, Thomas Cranmer, a man much affected by the radical theology of the would-be reformers, agreed to preside over a court which dissolved the royal marriage and enabled Henry to marry Anne Boleyn. The action seems to have fitted in excellently with the mood of the English people, more particularly the urban and merchant classes. Events that had occurred earlier in the reign had revealed how widespread anti-clericalism had become, how the mass of the people had but little respect for those whom they regarded as indolent monks, begging friars and unpatriotic prelates. There is no occasion here to analyse the causes of this anti-clericalism but in passing it may be noted that a great many people believed that the Church was exploiting the nation by transferring wealth to Rome, where it was used for secular purposes. The members of the upper middle class and many members of the nobility were well-satisfied to witness the discomfiture of the Church and its leaders in the hope that the pickings might be used to enrich their families. Finally, the leaven within the bread, the new ideas which challenged the supremacy of Rome and revealed, it was said, the insecure intellectual foundations on which its claims were built were spreading, especially in the universities. Religion and politics coalesced then to support the breach with Rome. The so-called Reformation Parliament of 1529–36 passed a series of Acts ensuring the royal control over the Church and cutting off links, financial and political, which bound England to Rome. The final more occurred in 1539 when all the remaining monasteries were closed; the monks were not on the whole badly treated for many received livings and some pensions, but their estates and endowments passed to the Crown. Now, there was nothing in all this which would necessarily have made the breach with Rome permanent. Henry, indeed, always remained a Roman Catholic at heart, critical of changes which his Protestant advisers would have liked to have brought about in the body of doctrine. The first stage of the Reformation in England was accomplished by a minority party, mainly for political reasons, but it was a decision in which the majority of the English people acquiesced. Henry died in 1547. His heir was a ten-year-old boy, his son by his third wife, Jane Seymour, precocious, interested in theological questions and educated as a convinced Protestant, but the real say in affairs rested successively with two great noblemen, Somerset and then Northumberland, both of whom were Protestants. Thus, while the spoliation of the Church continued apace throughout the short reign, the more Protestant of the Church leaders were able to manipulate changes of doctrine which cut England off from Rome more decisively than ever. Foreign scholars came to teach within the red brick of Cambridge and the grey stone of Oxford, injecting contemporary English scholarship with a dose of erudition and controversy. Edward's death in 1553 led to an abrupt change. His successor, the Princess Mary, was Henry's daughter by his first wife, a pious Roman Catholic, who had undoubtedly felt bitterly the changes which she had been compelled to witness during the past twenty years. That she had the ability and insight which made the Tudors so distinguished a family must be admitted, but she made an error of judgment when she married the greatest Catholic prince in Europe, the future Philip II of Spain, less because he was Catholic than because he was Spanish. Her religious policy which was, in fact, a reversion to the *status quo* was as unpopular as her husband. There can be little doubt that her death from dropsy in 1558 freed the country from the angry glare of civil strife which, following the flames of Smithfield market, would have gone a long way to wreck its precarious economic security.

The new Queen, Elizabeth, Mary's younger sister, was not by nature a devoutly religious woman, her religion was in fact partly governed by her politics, but her judgment was extraordinarily incisive and telling. Much as she might herself appreciate the pageantry and ritual of the Church from which her father had broken loose, she saw that a return to Roman Catholicism spelt political and diplomatic ruin. Too many of her advisers had a vested interest in maintaining the Protestant settlement while it was widely recognized that, apart from the higher clergy, there had been a great move away from Romanism in the past decade. Her accession had coincided, too, with the return of the exiles. Fervent, grave divines flocked from Strasburg and Frankfort, Basle and Geneva, imbued with so great a hatred of papistry and all that it stood for that they only awaited an opportunity to copy Calvin's work at Durham and Hereford, Westminster and Norwich. Elizabeth and her advisers saw which way the wind was blowing, but neither she nor they wished to create a settlement which would alienate any large body of her population. Trivial incidents

displayed the trend of events. At Christmas, 1558, the
Queen informed the celebrant, Bishop Oglethorpe, that he
must not elevate the Host at the High Mass, but the Bishop
was an honest man and after the Gospel the Queen rose
and swept out from the Chapel. On January 15th of the
new year the streets were thronged with people who had
come to catch a glimpse of the Coronation ceremonies; the
triumphal arch which had been erected in Cornhill emphasized the break from Rome. The Coronation service
itself showed how unstable the situation was, for while the
Mass was said in Latin, the Epistle and Gospel were read in
English and Latin. Ten days later, Parliament met. Mass
was sung in Westminster Abbey. Later the Queen was to
be escorted to her canopy, the rich coloured baldachino
by the High Altar, but Elizabeth, pungent as she could be,
informed the monks bearing the lit tapers: "Away with
those torches"—the tapers flicker and disappear—"for we
see very well." But what do we see? No one was quite
certain. The preacher, Dr. Cox, a returned exile, spent
ninety minutes in proving that the present system was
impious, but it did not need Dr. Cox to make Elizabeth or
Cecil decide that neither Henry VIII nor Edward VI had, in
fact, solved the problem of the future religion of the
country.

The "Via Media", the middle path of compromise,
which Elizabeth followed seems at first sight to be based
purely on political considerations. The Council sought to
create a Church system which would enable Catholic and
Protestant to worship together at the same altar so that they
would obey the same sovereign in secular and religious
matters. Neither the Bishops nor Convocation agreed to
accept the Council's recommendations, but this made no
difference, for it was Parliament and not Convocation
which passed the Act of Uniformity and the Act of Supremacy

which laid the foundations of the Elizabethan system. To impose this new system, Elizabeth nominated Matthew Parker, the lame Master of Corpus, Cambridge, to the archbishopric of Canterbury, a position which he only accepted with the greatest reluctance. And rightly, for it was with the greatest difficulty that he was able to bring some kind of stability to an unstable situation.

For all that Parker could do—and his appointment was a stroke of genius—the condition of the Church continued chaotic. All those who could, including the Queen herself, sought to deprive the Church of its property, in some cases of the leaden roofs of the churches and the metal of the bells. The clergy themselves, even after the deprivation of the Romanists, were ignorant, recalcitrant and disorderly, nor could any man be happy or certain as to the nature of the service which he was, under penalty of a fine, obliged to attend. Such a situation could not long endure without disaster. What made it worse was the continuing hold and expansion of the two opposition parties, the Roman Catholics without and the Puritans within the Church of England. The Roman Catholic squires remained fairly quiescent in the first half of the reign, realizing that toleration was the happy issue of loyalty. This was, however, an attitude which grew less common as the effects of the Counter-Reformation became more apparent in this country. Romish priests had fled abroad where they took an active part in training young, enthusiastic English Catholics to undertake missionary work in their own country. In 1570 the Pope had declared that Elizabeth was no longer the rightful sovereign, in effect, releasing all Roman Catholics from their allegiance and so throwing the cloak of treason over them. In the next thirty years while the attitude of the Government stiffened on the one side, the activities of the Roman Catholics became more and more prominent on the other. Loyola's response had come home to England. His priests, disguised as laymen, intrepid for the faith and gallant and adventurous in their vocation, travelled through the country, hiding in the houses of devout Roman Catholic squires, and within their shelter softly repeating the Mass.

The Roman Catholic danger was actually less than it might appear to be. It is probable that the reverse was true of the Puritan clergy who conducted their propaganda within the framework of the Church of England. Their devotion and sincerity were as unquestionable as those of the Roman missionary priests. They held that the Church in England had been too slack and lethargic in casting off the toils of outworn tradition. The matters about which they argued may seem trivial to us who hardly care whether a priest wears surplice, vestment or cassock, but to the contemporary mind such matters were of great symbolic importance. The richly coloured vestment or even the white surplice seemed to reflect a state of mind which placed more importance on ceremony and dress than on belief. What they wanted was the plain, black preaching gown which in its clear, straight flowing lines represented the gravity and clarity of faith. Everything which tended to reflect the worshipper from his subordination to the grace of God, or from his concentration on his duty to his neighbour were thus condemned, more particularly when they were closely associated with the ceremonies and ideas of the Roman Church, the use of the organ, the ring in marriage, genuflection, the crossing and kneeling which were typical of the age-old service. In these matters they seem to us to have mistaken incidentals for fundamentals. In reality, they realized that the focal-point of Calvinism was faith founded on the Scriptures. Everything which was in disagreement or not covered by the Scriptures was therefore thought to

be idolatrous and impious. The Bible became for the
Puritan the norm for doctrine and behaviour. If the Bible
said nothing about bishops or organs, then clearly bishops
and organs were later accretions for which there was no
necessity. If the Bible, especially the Old Testament, condemned witchcraft and upheld the observance of the
Sabbath, then as clearly witches were to be condemned
and Sunday (with which they were inclined to identify the
Jewish Sabbath) must be strictly kept. Stripped of all but
this Puritanism must seem inhuman and unattractive. It
should not, however, be forgotten that later Puritanism was
capable of attractive and sincere devotion and was as
representative of the supreme simplicity of divine love as
the Roman Catholics it opposed. Nor should it be
forgotten that the Puritan, as the heir of Calvin, was
catastrophically aware of his utter subordination before God
and his complete inability to save himself without the grace
of God. Such a realization was bound, by limiting the
human element, to give a steel-like element to Puritan
thought and conduct, which has proved unpleasing to the
humanist Christian.

Where did the Church of England stand in this crisis?
No one could say with the slightest degree of certainty.
The Queen herself liked Catholic ritual but was not by
nature a religious woman. Her archbishops represented
different points of view. Parker was a moderate, hoping
to enforce (by persuasion and charity), the compromise
which had been reached by the Acts of 1559. His successor,
Edmund Grindal, who had long presided over the diocese
of London, was a Puritan in theology and outlook; he spent
his last years in retirement and disgrace. John Whitgift,
the powerful master of Trinity who succeeded him, has been
described as the Queen's "little black father". He had
long been an out and out opponent of Puritanism, more

particularly at Cambridge where he had been responsible for depriving the Lady Margaret Professor, Thomas Cartwright, of his position for upholding Puritan views, but a close investigation of Whitgift's ideas on religious matters proves him in much to have been Calvinistical. Cecil criticized his methods because they savoured of the Spanish Inquisition. The Queen's other advisers, Leicester and Walsingham, openly favoured the Puritans, nor was the Episcopal Bench distinguished for the clarity or constancy of its views. It was a patchwork of time servers, statesmen and conscientious clergy, few of whom had very much understanding of the difficult crisis in which the Church was placed. If this was true of its leaders, how much more true was it of the rank and file. It is widely recognized that Shakespeare was the most representative dramatist of the age, but there is no sign of any real appreciation of the religious situation, and very little of religious belief, in his plays. If religion was a matter about which men spoke in the taverns of the city of London and in the gabled manor houses, it was obviously a religion whose form and meaning lacked a definite content unless one were either a Puritan or a Roman Catholic.

But a country parson had an answer. This is an astonishing and unique event; that a comparatively little-known and in many ways undistinguished man should have given the Anglican Church its most momentous apologia. Richard Hooker was the Thomas Aquinas of Anglicanism. What was more, both men were instinctively Catholic, in the sense that reason and faith determined their ideas and their attitude towards religious matters. Neither Aquinas nor Hooker ever received preferment in the usual sense of the word, a sure indication that it is not always possible to determine the extent of a man's influence by the position which he holds.

It is still possible to walk from the Bell Harry Tower of Canterbury through fields, apple orchards and country lanes to the little village of Bishopsbourne which lies a few miles away. It is here, where a great novelist, Joseph Conrad, lived so recently, that Hooker died and here that he wrote much of his great book, *The Laws of Ecclesiastical Polity*. He was not, one is given to understand, personally impressive. There was not that glint of enthusiasm which lit the eyes of Loyola or Francis with burning fire, or the impressive bulk of an Aquinas. He was a plain, scholarly little man, "judicious" is the adjective which has been rightly fastened on him. He was quiet and retiring, so that he found it difficult to look his pupils in the face. He was a slow-moving, meditative, scholar, ever fond of his books, nor need we, even if we dismiss on recent evidence the unhappiness of his marriage, feel that Izaak Walton was committing a mistake when he imagined that Hooker felt many of the trials of married life more than some men, being forced away from his books to assist the "necessary, household business" and to "rock the cradle". Walton thus describes his appearance at Bishopsbourne as that of "an obscure, harmless man; a man in poor clothes, his loins usually girt in a coarse gown, or canonical coat; of a mean stature, and stooping, and yet more lowly in the thoughts of his soul, his body worn out, not with age, but study and holy mortifications, his face full of heat pimples, begot by his inactivity and sedentary life."

This "judicious" Mr. Hooker was a Devonian by birth, born at Heavitree, now a suburb of Exeter, at the end of March, 1554. We know little of his ancestry, but Walton surmises that he soon showed a "questioning mind" and "a quick apprehension of many perplext parts of learning", so that he was able to gain the goodwill of his uncle, John Hooker. John was the friend of a very notable man, John

E

Jewel, a reformer whom Elizabeth had made Bishop of Salisbury and who had recently written a small book of the greatest importance, an *Apology* on behalf of the religious settlement. It was then only right that Jewel should have become, through his friendship with John Hooker, Richard's patron and protector. Through his good offices, Richard proceeded, presumably from what has since become Exeter School, to Corpus Christi College, Oxford.

It was inevitable that his Oxford career should be distinguished and finally crowned with a fellowship. He was admitted in 1568, elected to a scholarship in December, 1573, and became a Fellow in 1577, acting two years later for the Hebrew professor. In 1580 he was expelled from his fellowship, apparently for opposing Warwick's nominee, Dr. Barfoot, to the headship of the college, but was reinstated a month later. But these facts give no real indication of what Oxford meant to Hooker. In the first place, it made him fully acquainted with England and with the critical trends that were disturbing the even tenor of religious life and threatening to create chaos in the Church. Secondly, there was the continued close association with Bishop Jewel about which Izaak Walton tells us a characteristic story. Hooker had been ill at Oxford and on his recovery he broke his journey at Salisbury to visit the bishop. He dined with the bishop, looking out on that gem of loveliness, the Close and the Cathedral. Forgetting to give him any money when he left, Jewel recalled him and gave him "a walking staff" and ten groats to assist him on the road to Exeter. He promised Richard ten groats more if he returned the stick, which he had used in his travels in Germany, safe and sound. Before Hooker could do this, Jewel was dead. This not only deprived Hooker of a patron but deprived the Church of a man whom it could ill spare because he—and perhaps he alone—realized that the crisis of the period required an intellectual as well as an active response. In the event his Elijah's cloak was to fall with great success upon Hooker. But Jewel's death left him without a patron which was yet doubly necessary since his fellowship still stood six years away. Happily, fortune favoured him and brought him a new and influential friend in Edwin Sandys, the son of Bishop Sandys of London (later the Archbishop of York) to whom he acted as tutor. Sandys was about the same age as Hooker and always retained the greatest respect for his friend. And so life continued, serene, quiet, meditative; Hooker was ordained priest and continued constant in scholarship until the day that took him to preach at St. Paul's Cross.

Because so much has been written about Hooker's marriage, it requires some attention. Walton's account may be remembered. After the sermon at Paul's Cross, he went to the house of a draper, John Churchman (almost certainly, as the Merchant Taylors connections prove, through the friendship of the latter with the Bishop and Edwin Sandys). Hooker was wet and weary and was provided by Mrs. Churchman with a "warm bed, and rest and drink, proper for a cold". She also provided him with a wife "that might prove a nurse to him; such an one as might prolong his life and make it more comfortable". The marriage was, according to Walton, "ill-assorted", for Joan Churchman was compared to a "dripping house". In support of this, he cites the evidence of Sandys and his friend, George Cranmer who, visiting Hooker at his rectory at Drayton Beauchamp, "were forced to leave him to the company of his wife, Joan, and seek themselves a quieter lodging for the next night". Recent investigators, Dr. Sisson in particular, have proved that the marriage was far less disastrous than it has been made out to have been. It is indeed highly improbable that Hooker married Joan

Churchman at the time or date which Walton would give us. He was, in fact, married at St. Augustine's, Watling Street, on February 13th, 1588. In other words, Hooker remained "constant in scholarship" not only until he preached the sermon at Paul's Cross but for some considerable time after it, that is, if the evidence for the sermon itself is sufficient. There is not the remotest indication in any case that Mrs. Hooker was the nagging wife that historians have made her out to be. That her husband did not take kindly to domestic duties we may well believe but that Mrs. Hooker was a scold is far more difficult to accept. He names his wife as the sole executrix of his will. It is true that she married the Canterbury alderman, Edward Nethersole, less than a year after her husband's death, but this casts no reflection on her relations with her first husband. She lived at Stone Hall, in Wincheap, Canterbury until her death on February 18th, 1603.

Hooker continued then as a Fellow of Corpus Christi some time after 1581. Certainly the Mayor and Chamber of Exeter granted him a student's pension of £4 a year in 1582. In 1584 he was appointed vicar of Drayton Beauchamp, but there is no evidence that he lived there before his appointment to the relatively important post of Master of the Temple in succession to Dr. Alvey. The Temple was a preaching centre where the Puritan divine, Walter Travers, had already made his name as an exponent of the Puritan viewpoint. The post suited Hooker because it gave him an opportunity to put forward the ideas on the Anglican Church which were maturing as a result of his experience as scholar, student and priest. It seems probable that the house to which he was entitled as Master of the Temple was in such ill-repair that he could not live there, and that this was the occasion of his going to stay with the Churchmans in Watling Street. His friend, Sandys, was

living with the Churchmans from 1588 with a considerable
retinue, in addition to Mr. and Mrs. Hooker. It is highly
probable, certain indeed, that so much hospitality was one
of the factors that led to the breakdown of the city draper's
finances. Whatever the details of this, it is clear that
Hooker was now married and living in London.

And it was while he was in London that the idea of his
great book came to him and was planned. Walton's account
is that the idea germinated in his mind at the Temple and
that he spoke to the Archbishop about it: "I have not
only satisfied myself, but have began a Treatise, in which I
intend a justification of the Laws of our Ecclesiastical
Polity." This needs supplementing. The religious atmosphere of contemporary London was highly charged with
controversy and temper. In 1587 the Dean of Salisbury,
John Bridges, had published a most ponderous book, 1,412
pages long, directed against Calvinism, entitled, *A Defence
of the Government Established in the Church of England for
Ecclesiastical Matters,* printed, incidentally, by Richard
Hooker's own cousin, Windet. The Puritans replied in a
series of devastating pamphlets supposedly written by
"Martin Marprelate", "against right poisoned, persecuting,
and terrible priests . . . petty popes, proud prelates, in-
tolerable withstanders of reformation, enemies of the
gospel". If the stately Spanish galleons sailing towards the
English coast aroused greater interest than the Marprelate
tracts, it is no less true that, the greater danger over, the
ships lying timber-strewn on the Irish and Scottish rocks,
authority in Church and State turned their attention on this
menace to the Anglican Church. In 1593, three Puritan
dissenters, supposedly implicated in the Marprelate tracts,
were executed while Parliament passed an Act imposing
severe penalties on "seditious sectaries". But it is one
thing to act energetically and another to justify one's action

to intelligent men and women. What was this Church of England in whose defence the authorities in Church and State were acting with such energy? It was not easy to answer this question with any degree of precision, but the Master of the Temple had long been concerned with the problem. The result surpassed—at any rate from the view of later generations—all expectations. At last the Anglican Church had an apologist who knew his ground—the *Laws of the Ecclesiastical Polity* began to be written.

The remainder of Hooker's life is inseparable from the massive work. It was begun in the crowded house in Watling Street, the first volume being complete at the end of December, 1592. In the previous year he had been offered and had accepted the living of Boscombe from the Bishop of Salisbury, actually in exchange with Nicholas Baldgay who succeeded him at the Temple. Walton surmised that Hooker told the Archbishop: "My Lord, when I lost the freedom of my cell, which was my college; yet I found some degree of it in my quiet country parsonage; but I am weary of the noise and oppositions of this place, and indeed God and nature did not intend me for contentions, but for study and quietness." The last point is true but it is probable that, despite his resignation at the Temple, Hooker continued to live at the Churchman residence in Watling Street or at Enfield, rather than at Boscombe. It was not until 1594 that he finally left London for Bishopsbourne where he remained until his death in 1600. When Hooker had completed the manuscript of the first volume he found some difficulty in finding a printer because "bookes of that argument and on that parte were not saleable". This suggests that printers were chary of undertaking long and ponderous works of apologetic which had far fewer readers than the more abusive pamphlets still circulating freely from the underground Puritan press. So depressed was Hooker by this disappointing conclusion that his friend, Edwin Sandys, offered to print the book at his own expense. The printer was Hooker's cousin, John Windet, the son of Hooker's aunt, Anne. It is clear that Sandys stood to lose on the transaction as he had to bear the cost of the printing and the paper. The first book was published by Windet in 1593 but the evidence suggests only sold very slowly. Five of the eight books were, in fact, published before Hooker's death in 1600, but the three remaining volumes did not appear until 1648 and 1661 respectively. Why was this? It certainly constitutes a minor mystery to which there seems only one probable solution, that the Anti-Calvinist nature of the contents proved unacceptable to Hooker's friend and executor, Edwin Sandys, and therefore prevented their publication.

Hooker died in 1600. "He fell into a long and sharp sickness, occasioned by a cold taken in his passage by water betwixt London and Gravesend . . . yet all this time he was solicitous in his study." His will, which was proved on December 3rd, 1600, shows that his estate was valued at £1,092 9s. 2d., accumulated largely, one learns, through the efforts of his "trusty servant, Thomas Lane, that was wiser than his master in getting money for him and more frugal than his mistress in keeping it". He left his widow as residuary legatee and £100 each to his four daughters, Alice, Cecily, Jane and Margaret. It was doubly unfortunate that there should have been such an amount of litigation as the direct and indirect sequel to Hooker's death, for the little that we know of him personally shows clearly that he was essentially the unassuming, scholarly priest who is in many ways the glory of the Anglican Church.

It may appear strange that a man whose life was in many ways so ordinary and who never, so far as we know, was faced with a great decision or a dramatic crisis in his life, should have been included in this series of essays. The buttercup-strewn fields of Bishopsbourne and the draper's house at Watling Street seem so far removed from the heated atmosphere of Hippo, of the lecturing halls of Cologne, or the Gregorian College, or even from Mr. Wesley's preaching tours. And yet this quiet little, stooping priest was in his own way as great a man and contributed as much to the religious life of the world as Augustine or Wesley. He, too, was confronted by a crisis which threatened to result in the disintegration of Christian society and of Anglicanism in particular. And in response he offered a solution in the *Laws of Ecclesiastical Polity*.

What was the nature of the solution offered to the world by Hooker? It was in some ways the sequel, far less technically perfect or comprehensive, to the *Summa Theologica*. For if Hooker has neither the massive erudition or clarity of Aquinas, his books yet deserve attention as a *livre de circonstance* of permanent merit. Designed principally to refute the ideas of Church Government and the Scriptures put forward by Thomas Cartwright and his Puritan followers, the book has an importance which far out-classes its immediate object.

Hooker emphasized the continuity of the Anglican Church. Unlike his more acutely Protestant contemporaries, he found in the faith of his own Church the true heir to medieval tradition, nor did he censure as harshly as they the teaching of medieval theologians. Indeed, his indebtedness both to St. Augustine and St. Thomas Aquinas was considerable. The Anglican Church was in conformity with the writings of the fathers, the decisions of great councils, and with the Christian tradition until it was perverted by the Romans. After an examination of the ministry of the Anglican Church he thus concludes: "I may securely therefore conclude that there are at this way in the Church

of England no other than the same degrees of ecclesiastical
order, namely, Bishops, Presbyters and Deacons, which had
their beginning from Christ and His Blessed Apostles
themselves.'' Anglicanism was thus intellectually and
spiritually in the main stream of Christian development and
the true heir to the spiritual culture of the past.

Hence the insistence on the organic nature of the Church
which appears throughout his book. Founded by Christ,
and moulded by the Apostles, fathers and early popes, the
Church was yet an ever unfinished product. He makes a
careful and important distinction between the fundamentals
and accessories of the faith. The Church, standing by its
fundamentals, must yet adapt itself to the spiritual needs of
every different age. It is rooted in the same soil and
possesses the same outward characteristics, but the bloom
has never the same shade of colour. The corporate
Church is an organism which may not be cut off from its
parent roots lest it may perish, but at the same time it can
grow upward into new forms. This is the whole nature of
Hooker's essential answer to the crisis of his times. He is
far less concerned with the abuses of the Church, the
existence of which had been recognized by all intelligent
Roman Catholics, than with the basic errors perpetuated by
the Roman Church, the nature and characteristics of the
Petrine headship, the inerrancy of the Pontiff and the
Church, and ultimately its devolution along paths which
were not in accord with the general tendency of past
tradition, more simply because there were suckers on the
organism depriving the plant of strength and energy and
damaging its beauty. ''Two things there are'', he said,
''which trouble greatly these later times; one that the
Church of Rome cannot, another that Geneva will not, err.''

A great deal of religious controversy turned round the
ultimate reliance which the believer was forced to give to

reason or faith. Towards the close of the Middle Ages, many scholars, following Occam and Scotus, had criticized the synthesis which Aquinas had formulated. There was also a more pronounced movement towards mystical theology. Life was a closed book which it was impertinent to try to open; except through meditation and concentration the Christian would be unable to pierce the "cloud of unknowing" or to lose himself in the ineffable heights of sublime and all-absorbing love. Both tendencies greatly influenced Protestant thinkers who were, in general, contemptuous of reason. Luther, with the fire of emotion burning in his soul, and Calvin, with his clear, crystal logic, held that the medieval reliance on reason was ludicrous, nay, impertinent and blasphemous. Hooker treated the whole problem with typical clarity. "Two opinions therefore there are concerning the sufficiency of Holy Scripture, each entirely opposite unto the other, and both repugnant unto truth. The schools of Rome teach Scripture to be so unsufficient, as if, except traditions were added, it did not contain all revealed and supernatural truth, which absolutely is necessary for the children of men in this life to know that they may in the next be saved. Others justly condemning this opinion grow likewise unto a dangerous extremity, as if Scripture did not only contain all things in that kind necessary, but all things simply, and in such sort that to do all things according to any other law were not only unnecessary but even opposite unto salvation, unlawful and sinful." And again: "The fourth degree of inducements is by fashioning the very notions and conceits of men's minds in such sort that when they read the Scriptures they may think that everything soundeth towards the advancement of that discipline and to the utter disgrace of the contrary . . ." He saw more clearly than his Puritan opponents that to abnegate the power of the human reason was in some sense to criticize the work of the Creator. Man is indeed minutely insignificant beside the awful presence of God, but God does not think man insignificant. In giving man a mind he has endowed him with that which may lead to the approach of divine truth. "By reason man attained unto the knowledge of things that are and are not sensible."

Richard Hooker therefore denied that the Scriptures alone constituted the sole guide to God, or that revelation, emphatically essential as it was to the faith, was the only way in which God manifested His will to the world. "So I trust that to mention what the Scripture of God leaveth unto the Church's discretion in some things is not in anything to impair the honour which the Church of God yieldeth to the sacred Scriptures' perfection. . . . Sundry things may be lawfully done in the Church, so as they be not done against the Scripture, although no Scripture do command them, but the Church, only following the light of reason, judge them to be in discretion meet." He acknowledged, then, that the Scriptures were completely essential to the Church but he also held that man's reason, interpreted differently through the ages, was equally valid a factor in revealing the mind of God. "Goodness", he said, "is seen with the eye of understanding. And the light of that eye is reason." Reason is, in fact, the complement of the Bible in informing man of God's will. "God being the author of Nature, her voice is but his instrument." "The law of Reason or human Nature is that which men by discourse of natural Reason have rightly found out themselves to be all for ever bound unto in their action."

What Hooker had done then was to adapt the medieval synthesis to modern conditions. He was, in many ways, a man of his times, particularly in his attitude to monarchy. Yet he was, above all, interested in proving that Anglicanism was as Catholic as the Church of Rome, indeed more so.

He referred back to past traditions and traditional beliefs and ceremonies, but he was also equally concerned with providing for the organic growth of the Church. Fundamentally, the most important contribution which Hooker made to contemporary thought was his emphasis on the natural law, the eternal reason of God made manifest through the laws of the Church and State as long as they did not contravene its injunctions. "All things, therefore, do work after a sort according to law; all other things according to a law, whereof some superior, unto Whom they are subject, is Author; only the works and operations of God have Him both for their Worker, and for the law whereby they are wrought. The being of God is a kind of law to His working; for that perfection which God is, giveth perfection to that which He doeth." It is this natural law of God, "whose seat is the bosom of God, whose voice the harmony of the law", which is represented both in the Scriptures and in man's reason. It forms the basis of the Church. It is the standard by which the laws of the State may be judged, on which the relations of society finally rest. It was in this way that Hooker's book became far more than the ephemeral study that it might have been. In addition to providing a response to the crisis which threatened to split Anglicanism, the Oxford scholar and country parson had written what may be judged the most masterly apologia on behalf of the Church of England that has ever been penned, a book of permanent value for the Christian community. The book may not have sold particularly well, but its reputation spread far beyond the English border. If we may believe Anthony à Wood, the Pope, Clement VIII, expressed his tribute in moving words: "There is no learning that this man hath not searched into, nothing too hard for his understanding. . . . His books will get reverence by age, for there are in them such seeds of eternity, that, if the rest be like this, they shall last till the last fire shall consume all learning.''

Scholars, Izaak Walton tells us, used after passing through Bridge, to leave the main Dover Road and turn into the quiet rectory of Bishopsbourne. And it becomes any Englishman to do the same:

> "*Yet he that lay so long obscurely low*
> *Doth now preferr'd to greater honours go.*
> *Ambitious men, learn hence to be more wise;*
> *Humility is the true way to rise:*
> *And God in me this lesson did inspire,*
> *To bid this humble man, Friend, sit up higher.*"

BOOKS FOR FURTHER READING

R. Hooker, *The Laws of Ecclesiastical Polity* (ed. J. Keble, 3 vols., 1836; Rev. R. W. Church and F. Paget, Oxford, 1888).

F. Paget, *An Introduction to the Fifth Book of Hooker's treatise of the Laws of Ecclesiastical Polity*, 2nd. ed., 1908.

Izaak Walton, *Richard Hooker*, ed. Sampson, 1913.

L. S. Thornton, *The Theology of Richard Hooker*, 1924.

A. P. D'Entrèves, *Medieval Contribution to Political Thought*, 1939.

A. P. D'Entrèves, *Richard Hooker*, 1932. (In Italian.)

C. J. Sisson, *The Marriage of the Judicious Mr. Hooker*, 1940.

E. T. Davies, *The Political Ideas of Richard Hooker*, 1946.

VII. John Wesley

THE ATTRACTION of eighteenth-century society is undeniable, even if its obvious defects are recognized, its extreme class-consciousness, its poverty and its crudity. As against this, there was a calm, a courtesy revealed in the lifting of tricorned hats and in prayers at heavily-cushioned desks. An observer looking back at the age from his own disquietening period feels something of its sober complacency as he reads contemporary letters and diaries: One glint of sunlight drifting through glass on to rich carpets and delicately-carved furniture. Read, if you will, the diaries of English country clergymen of the eighteenth century, and above all, that of Parson Woodforde. There is a scent about them of new-mown hay and briar roses, of evenings spent at manor houses, good food, the smell of leather saddles and hunting boots, all the inborn quietness and charm of a countryside which has so nearly disappeared, of sermons and occasional services and visiting. From this picture one thing alone was lacking, divine enthusiasm. All those whose characters we have so far portrayed would, with the exception of the one man who was himself a country parson, have found the atmosphere of the countryside alien to their modes of thought, and the religious customs and experience of the contemporary church sterile. And this would have meant far more to them than the actual abuses which characterized the eighteenth-century church, its pluralities, its non-residence, its highly paid prelates and poorly paid curates, the close association between the bench of bishops and the Government. All these facts were true to a greater or lesser extent, but they were incidental to the real problem, the lack of depth in the vocation of the ordinary English parson. There were certainly exceptions, but mere conscientious performance of duty, the existence of worldliness stained by saintliness, prayer and communion could not make up for lack of enthusiasm. There are some, who find enthusiasm crude, and yet mainly because it is a primitive and fundamental emotion it is inseparable from Christianity. The sanity of the scholar, the conscientiousness of bishop and parish priest, the essential reasonableness of the Christian gospel, which give an undeniable attraction to the Georgian Church, were without avail as long as enthusiasm for a high calling was absent.

Thus religion in the eighteenth century in England was in a state of crisis. The wind of strife, which had ruffled the waters so repeatedly in the previous period had died down and left a smooth pond, in some danger of stagnation. The comfortable calm pervaded the English Dissenting and Roman Catholic communities as well as the Church of England, but it was the Church of England which was most affected by the trend of events. There was a real danger that it might have settled down into an Erastian institution possessing no real corporate life of its own apart from the State which its leaders upheld. It was this response which John Wesley tried to meet and, in spite of the secession of the Wesleyan groups, provided successfully for the Church. As a result of Wesley's work, and that of those who followed him, Anglicanism emerged stronger and more aware of its calling.

The environment in which John Wesley grew up did much to form his personality. His father was Samuel Wesley, a Lincolnshire country parson, who had deserted the Dissent, in which he had passed many years of his life, for High Anglicanism. If he hoped for preferment he was doomed to disappointment, for going to the low, marshy village of Epworth in 1697, he remained vicar there until his death in 1735. Nor was he a particularly successful parish priest. His parishioners disliked him and on occasions showed themselves actively hostile towards him. He spent his time in writing books that were not worth reading and poems which never rose to distinction. But it is possible that poetry formed a means of escapist expression in a drab environment, and it may be that the romantic emotionalism of John Wesley can be traced back to his father. John's mother, the mother of his eighteen brothers and sisters, was far more distinguished in character and ability than her husband. Her father, Dr. Annesley, was a scholarly dissenting minister from whom she inherited much of her unswerving, rather narrow faith. It is clear that Mrs. Susanna Wesley remained the dominant influence in the life of the young son whom she determined to dedicate to the Lord.

His early career must have left its mark upon John. If he was not, as he must at times have been, definitely unhappy, he must have felt strongly the pervading hostility of the villagers and the incompetence of his father. He must have compared this with the iron will of his mother who found time to instruct her children in the rudiments of knowledge as well as to undertake the many cares and chores of the big household. "Dear Son," she told John later, "The children were always put in a regular method of living, in such things as they were capable of, from their birth. . . . When turned a year old (and some before) they were taught to fear the rod and to cry softly. . . . They were so constantly used to eat and drink what was given them that when any of them was ill there was no difficulty in making them take the most unpleasant medicine; for they durst not refuse it, though some of them would presently throw it up. . . . They were very early made to distinguish the Sabbath from other days,

before they could well speak or go. . . . There was no such
thing as loud playing or talking allowed of, but everyone
was kept close to business for the six hours of school.'' If
the poetry of the father was neither lacking in the lives of
John and of his brother, Charles, the mother's force of will
was the decisive factor in the character of the elder of the
two brothers.

John Wesley was born in 1703. He was educated at
Charterhouse and at Christ Church; in 1726 he was elected
a Fellow of Lincoln College, Oxford. Early eighteenth-
century Oxford was neither stimulating to the intellect nor
to the soul. If its reputation for learning was still considerable, the mass of its dons spent their time in disputing
querulous scholastic points of no conceivable importance or
in port-drinking and cards until a suitable living in the gift
of the college they adorned fell vacant. There was little
enough food for mind or soul; even the body, unless one
dined at High Table, sometimes lacked quality and susten-
ance. It was to this Oxford, not yet enriched by the work
of Hawksmoor and the other great architects of the period,
that Wesley went in 1720, nor were there as yet any signs of
a change in his own attitude to life. But he did not waste his
time. He read the early fathers of the Church and some of
the classic devotional literature, in particular à Kempis, the
seventeenth-century writer, Jeremy Taylor, and his own
elder contemporary, William Law, author of the *Serious
Call*. "I shall", wrote one whom he admired, "apply
myself to read such books . . . as warm, kindle and enlarge
the soul; as being convinced of every day's experience
that I have more need of heat than light." John was
himself much more concerned with warmth than with
illumination, with passionate enthusiasm than scholarly
exposition. His reading and his general thought, not
untouched by his mother's devotion and earlier teaching,

convinced him that contemporary society was un-Christian, that the university and the city in which it stood were singularly lacking in the reconciliation of the conventional teaching of the schools with the active practice of Christianity. In November, 1729, John Wesley and three others, his brother Charles, who was at Christ Church, Morgan of the same college and Kirkham of Merton "began to spend some evenings a week in reading, chiefly the Greek Testament", thus founding what was dubbed by contemporaries the "Holy Club" or the Methodists. This little group sought to reinvigorate the life of the university with the practice of Christianity, with the reception of the Holy Communion, with a regular prayer life, with visiting the Oxford gaol, and charity. John never forsook the habits which he formed as a young Oxford don, even if he, to some extent, lost the High Anglican tradition in which they took their shape.

Oxford could not, however, meet that unease which ate at his mind. Where was true peace to be found, the peace of a soul that passed understanding? Mutual admiration for à Kempis' writings made him a frequent visitor to Sally Kirkham, the daughter of the rector of Stanton, a charming Cotswold village, but this dalliance with Varanese, as he christened her, was closed by her marriage with the local schoolmaster. It was not under the steeples of Oxford or the fresh green of Cotswold fields that John was to find true peace of mind. While he continued vaguely uneasy as to his future, he received an invitation to go as a missionary to the new colony of Georgia founded through the beneficence of General Oglethorpe. John and his brother Charles embarked on the *Simmonds* at Gravesend on October 14th, 1735.

This Tuesday embarkation was an epochal event in the Wesleys' lives, even if the Georgian adventure seemed disastrous. This is not surprising. The new colony had been founded originally to house poor debtors who suffered through no fault of their own from the stringency of English law. But other factors affected the character of the young state, its proximity to the Spanish American frontier and to the slave colonies. Oglethorpe soon had more than he could cope with as a result of the colonists' quarrels. In the midst of this heated, adventurous colony there came two staid and prim young men, inexperienced in the ways of the world and enthusiastic in carrying the ideas of the Oxford Methodists into southern America. That way, surely, lay disaster, as events soon revealed. When Charles found that a certain Dr. Hawkins fired off a gun inopportunely near to his person, he had the doctor imprisoned, an event which so shocked the medico's wife that she had a miscarriage. Charles had then to suffer the additional ignominy of another gunshot, this time fired by the irate lady. He soon showed such a lack of discretion and good sense that Oglethorpe was profoundly relieved when he embarked for England. But John was still left behind to carry on the tradition of severe discipline and rigid churchmanship which had made his brother so unpopular. Unfortunately, John was of a romantic nature and fell in love with Sophy Hopkey. The attempt to combine rigid discipline with romance was foredoomed to fail. Wesley could not make up his mind whether the Lord willed his marriage to the delicious Sophy or not. "Miss Sophy," he said, "I should think myself happy if I was to spend my life with you," but Sophy could not wait for ever for the Lord's decision and married Mr. Williamson. Wesley was so hurt that he took the unprecedented step of refusing to admit Sophy to Communion. Such a step was calamitous. Wesley suffered imprisonment, eventually managed to escape from the colony by the *Samuel* en route for England.

The Georgian experience, disastrous as it might have been, proved of the greatest significance, for it had brought the Wesleys into contact with a German Protestant sect known as the Moravian brethren. Since 1737 this Pietist group had their headquarters at Herrnhut, eighteen miles south-east of Bautzen, under the lead of a cultured noble-man, Count Zinzendorf. They had proved earnest and successful missionaries, in Greenland, in Surinam, Georgia, Pennsylvania and Santa Cruz, their simplicity and gentle piety making a profound appeal to the religiously minded man. John had been particularly impressed by their behaviour on the *Simmonds* going out to Georgia. In a storm they had remained undismayed and unshaken, singing hymns among themselves until the seas became calmer. Charles' own hymns represented the melody and poetry which so often marked their songs. On his return from Georgia, John was again brought into contact with the Moravians and, through the influence of Peter Böhler, became a member of the Moravian church at Fetter Lane, London, in 1738.

But he still felt insecure, felt that his faith lacked the conviction, the certainty of salvation which he had noticed in his Moravian companions. Both brothers must have realized that their Georgian experiment had not resounded to the credit of the Church and they were depressed by their apparent failure to make contact with spiritual reality. They were aware of the abuses which characterized the Church of their day and wished to provide the Church with a stimulus which would arouse the religious enthusiasm of the people, but they could not do so unless they themselves felt absolutely convinced of the reality of the message which they were to preach. Psychologically, their minds were prepared for "conversion". It is a long call from the scene in the Milan garden to Georgian London in 1738, but the nature of the experience which Augustine and John and Charles Wesley endured was similar—the sudden, dramatic realization which changed and framed the whole future course of their life. Charles Wesley suddenly found "conversion" as his friends stood around his bedside—he was ill on Whitsunday, 1738, noting down later the meaning of the experience which he had undergone:

> "*Where shall my wondering soul begin?*
> *How shall I all to heaven aspire?*
> *A slave redeemed from death and sin,*
> *A brand plucked from eternal fire,*
> *How shall I equal triumph raise*
> *Or sound my great Deliverer's praise.*"

Less than three days later his brother was able to record in his journal a similar experience: "In the evening I went very unwillingly to a society in Aldersgate Street, where one was reading Luther's preface to the Epistle to the Romans. About a quarter before nine, while he was describing the change which God works in the heart through faith in Christ, I felt my heart strangely warmed. I felt I did trust in Christ, Christ alone, for salvation, and an assurance was given me that He had taken away *my* sins, even *mine* and saved *me* from the law of sin and death." The long spiritual experience which had begun in his Oxford days had reached its consummation.

The outstanding point about greatness in religious biography seems to revolve around the pursuit of one object, predominating and overshadowing all future existence, once the great decision has been taken. Augustine turned to the *City of God*, Francis to the ideals of his order and Thomas to the great *Summa Theologica*, Calvin to the model state of Geneva, Loyola to the Society of Jesus and Hooker to the

Laws of Ecclesiastical Polity. Once the decision has been taken there can be no turning back nor can there be the remotest deviation from the main, controlling object. This was equally true of John Wesley. He still had fifty-three years of life in front of him in 1738. He retained his health, his wits, his intelligence, to the end. There is no more charming portrait of him than the pen and ink sketch of him walking arm in arm with his two friends in the last year or so of his life. And every single day was spent in unceasing activity. Over the rough roads of England, Wales and Scotland, on horseback he rode through darkening evenings and early mornings towards some place where the message could be preached. As the clergy of the Church of England looked more and more askance at the unusual method of Wesley's organization, the open fields became the centres of his congregations. Thousands who had never graced the inside of a church or listened to a preacher, heard the melodious, deeply-moving words of John Wesley. Contemporary accounts show how affecting, even hysterical, some of these meetings were. "I was like a wandering bird, cast out of the nest, till Mr. John Wesley came to preach his first sermon in Moorfields. Oh, that was a blessed morning for my soul! . . . When he had done, I said, 'This man can tell the secrets of my heart; he hath not left me there, for he hath showed the remedy, even the blood of Jesus'." The *Journal* which Wesley wrote contains a number of passages where the account reveals a degree of hysteria and excitement alien to the modern temperament. Within a year of his own "conversion", he was recording: "But although they saw signs and wonders . . . yet many would not believe. . . . To-day, Monday, 21, our Lord answered for Himself; for while I was enforcing these words, 'Be still, and know that I am God', he began to make bare his arm, not in a close room, nor in private, but

in the open air, and before more than two thousand wit-
nesses. One, and another, and another, was struck to the
earth; exceedingly trembling at the presence of his power.
Others cried, with a loud and bitter cry, 'What must we do
to be saved?' And in less than an hour seven persons,
wholly unknown to me until that time, were rejoicing and
singing, and with all their might, giving thanks to the God
of their salvation.'' But this response was mild beside what
happened at other meetings which Wesley recorded with
profound appreciation, if at times some misgiving, in his
Journal. The activities of John Berridge, the Anglican vicar
of Everton, seem to have been particularly effective at
working on the congregation: "The text was 'Having a
form of godliness, but denying the power thereof'. When
the power of religion began to be spoken of, the presence
of God really filled the place. And while poor sinners felt
the sentence of death in their souls, what sounds of distress
did I hear! The greatest number of them who cried or fell
were men; but some women, and several children, felt the
power of the same Almighty Spirit, and seemed just sinking
into hell. This occasioned a mixture of various sounds;
some shrieking, some roaring aloud. The most general was
a loud breathing, like that of people half strangled and
gasping for life; and indeed almost all the cries were like
those of human creatures dying in bitter anguish. Great
numbers wept without any noise; others fell down as dead;
some sinking in silence; some with extreme noise and
violent agitation.'' After the service had ended, they
returned to Mr. Berridge's house, where similar symptoms
seemed to exhibit themselves; "Immediately after, a
stranger, well-dressed, who stood facing me, fell backward
to the wall; then forward on his knees, wringing his hands
and roaring like a bull. His face at first turned quite red,
then almost black. He rose, and ran against the wall, till

Mr. Keeling and another held him. He screamed out 'O what shall I do, what shall I do? O for one drop of the blood of Christ!' As he spoke, God set his soul at liberty; he knew his sins were blotted out; and the rapture he was in seemed too great for human nature to bear. He had come forty miles to hear Mr. Berridge.'' The number of occasions on which Wesley's own preaching evoked scenes of this description seemed to have been relatively infrequent, but this dramatic, semi-hysterical form of religious ecstasy was closely associated with the movement. ''During our prayer'', he noted on one occasion, ''one of them fell into a violent agony; but soon after began to cry out with confidence ' *My* Lord and *My* God.' '' The emotionalism of the movement is reflected in what Wesley tells of a visit which he paid to the school he had established at Kingswood in September, 1770. Most of the children ''went to see the body of Francis Evans, one of our neighbours, who died two or three days before. About seven, Mr. Hindmarsh met them all in the schools, and gave an exhortation suited to the occasion. He then gave out that hymn,

> *'And am I born to die,*
> *To lay this body down?*
> *And must my trembling spirit fly*
> *Into a world unknown?'*

This increased their concern, so that it was with great difficulty that they contained themselves till he began to pray. Then Al....r M...r and R....d N....e cried aloud for mercy; and quickly another and another, till all but two or three were constrained to do the same; and as long as he continued to pray, they continued the same loud and bitter cry.'' But this was not the end of the matter. The next day, Wednesday, the 19th, Wesley records: ''At the morning prayer many of them cried out again, though not so violently." Notices of a similar nature occur on all the following days, with the entry for the following Saturday, the 29th: "I was waked between four and five, by the children vehemently crying to God. The maids went to them at five. And first one of the boys, then another, then one and another of the maids, earnestly poured out their souls before God, both for themselves and for the rest. They continued weeping and praying till nine o'clock, not thinking about meat or drink; nay, Richard Piercy took no food all the day, but remained in words or groans calling upon God." This feast of religious emotion was consummated on the Sunday when "Eight of the children, and the three maids, received the Lord's Supper for the first time; and hitherto they are all rejoicing in God, and walking worthy of the Gospel." Poor Richard Piercy, the childish sobs reveal how lacking in intellectual compulsion much of Wesley's teaching was. If you were ready for grace, then God would surely endow your soul with it. "At Weaver's Hall, seven or eight persons were constrained to roar aloud, while the sword of the Spirit was 'dividing asunder their souls and spirits, and joints and marrow'. But they were all relieved upon prayer, and sang 'praises unto our God, and unto the Lamb that liveth for ever and ever'."

But it would be wrong to think of Wesley as a religious revivalist who hypnotized his listeners with his persuasive and melodious speech by appealing to their emotions. The *Journal* tells of the daily round of preaching and the careful supervision of the organization which was, almost in spite of himself, in the course of construction. He had soon found that clerical opposition, quite apart from the large numbers of his congregations, obliged him to preach in the open air. He thus notes the beginning of this: "At four in the afternoon, I submitted to be more vile, and proclaimed in the highways the glad tidings of salvation, speaking from a little eminence in a ground adjoining to the city to about three thousand people." But opposition from clergy and people was consistent and continuous. Visiting his father's old parish of Epworth, he found that the curate, Mr. Romilly, was actively hostile, saying in the course of his afternoon sermon: "one of the most dangerous ways of quenching the spirit was by enthusiasm". John therefore used his father's tomb as a preaching place and "found such a congregation as I believe Epworth never saw before".   Perturbed as old Samuel would have been by his son's unseemly behaviour, the poet in him would have been touched by the romantic nature of the appeal. Opposition was much worse elsewhere. "Not only the court and the alleys", he wrote of a visit to Bristol, "but all the street, upwards and downwards, was filled with people, shouting, cursing, and swearing, and ready to swallow the ground with fierceness and rage." At Pensford they drove a bull which they had been baiting upon him, but the poor bloody beast showed more sense than the degraded mob. "From three in the afternoon until past seven, the mob of Cork marched in grand procession, and then burnt me in effigy near Dant's Bridge," and two days later he noted: "The mob was still patrolling the streets abusing all that were called Methodists, and threatening to murder them, and pull down their houses if they did not leave this way."   But Wesley had never been lacking in either courage or persistency.   He laboured on with un-ceasing patience and left behind him a nucleus of faithful adherents who carried the faith further afield to their own immediate neighbourhood.

The greater part of the *Journal* contains descriptions of the two hundred and fifty thousand miles of journeying through England, Wales and Scotland and across the sea to

Ireland, mainly on horseback or later by chaise. This, too, was not without its difficulties; "presently after preaching I took horse. The rain obliged us to make haste; but in a while the saddle came over his neck, and then turned under his belly. I had then only to throw myself off, or I must have fallen under him. I was a little bruised, but soon mounted again, and rode to Lympsham, and the next day to Bristol". He was then in his sixty-eighth year. Gradually the net of his organization extended. In 1743 he opened his mission at Newcastle, the beginning of a great extension of Methodism in Yorkshire. Eight years later he first visited Scotland; he had already made his mark in Cornwall where his influence was very considerable and in Ireland. In 1784 a Methodist Chapel was built in New York. Forty years earlier the first Methodist conference had met. All this was highly significant but it pales beside the common-place detail of the *Journal*. Monday, August 25th, 1755, found him riding over the Cornish Moors to Looe, and thence to Fowey where "a little company met us, and conducted us to Luxillian. Between six and seven, I preached. . . . The congregation was large and deeply serious. But it was still larger on Tuesday evening, and several seemed to be cut to the heart. On Wednesday, they flocked from all parts. And with what eagerness did they receive the word? Surely many of these last will be first!" The Thursday found him at St. Mewan's: "I do not remember ever to have seen the yard in which I stood quite full before; but it would not now contain the congregation; many were obliged to stand without the gate. At five in the morning I preached at St. Austle's, to more than our Room could contain. In the evening I was at St. Ewe. One or two felt the edge of God's sword, and sunk to the ground; and indeed it seemed as if God would suffer none to escape Him; as if He both heard and answered our prayer:

'Dart into all the melting flame
of love, and make the mountains flow'."

"Dart into all the melting flame of love." It was this very flame of love which spurred the preacher on and on and ever onwards. "Between five and six in the evening we reached Minehead" (from Crediton), runs an earlier entry, and with the moors and North Hill behind and the small port and the sea in front, "about seven I preached near the seashore, to almost all the inhabitants of the place. Most of the gentlemen of the town were there, and behaved with seriousness and decency". One would wish to know if the Rev. Mr. Moggridge, the vicar of St. Michael's, Minehead, from 1709 to 1763, was there to compare the numbers gathered on the seashore with his regular congregation. Next day he crossed over into Wales and "I preached at six, and at five in the morning." One last illustration is taken from his journey to Wales in 1779 when he was in his seventy-seventh year: "Tues. 24. (Aug). Setting out immediately after preaching, about eight, I preached at Kidwelly . . . to a very civil and unaffected congregation. At eleven, though the sun was intensely hot, I stood at the end of the churchyard at Llanelly, and took occasion, from a passing bell, strongly to enforce these words: 'It is appointed unto men once to die.' About six I preached at Swansea to a large congregation without feeling any weariness. Wed. 25. I preached at five, and about eight in the Town-hall at Neath. In the afternoon I preached in the church near Bridge-End, to a larger congregation than I ever saw there before; and at six in the Town-hall at Cowbridge, much crowded, and hot enough. The heat made it a little more difficult to speak; but, by the mercy of God, I was no more tired when I had done, than when I rose in the morning. Thurs. 26. I preached at five, and again at eleven. I think this was the happiest time of all. The poor and the rich seemed to be equally affected. O how are the times changed at Cowbridge, since the people compassed the house where I was, and poured in stones from every quarter! But my strength was then according to my day; and, blessed be God, so it is still." The last entry of the diary, two sermons at Spitalfields and St. Paul's, Shadwell, occurs on Sunday, October 24th, 1790. If the diary ended, his work did not; on February 23rd, 1791, he preached his last sermon to a small company at Leatherhead on the text: "Seek ye the Lord while He may be found; call ye upon Him while He is near." He died on March 2nd following, with the word "Farewell" on his lips.

Wesley had his limitations. His affectionate nature which had involved him in a disastrous flirtation with Sophy Hopkey again led him into a romance with a girl eminently fitted to be his wife, Grace Murray, but he could come to no decision and by a rebound was brought into a more unsatisfactory marriage with a shrewish widow, Mary Vazeille, who tired of the continual travelling which marriage with Wesley entailed. At times he showed himself far too domineering in the conduct of his organization. Finally, the Wesleyan movement was fundamentally emotional. Lacking a sense of corporate churchmanship and so seized with the idea of making men into Christians that he ignored the traditions upon which Christianity was itself historically dependent, Wesley, in spite of himself, was forced away from the Church of England. The Wesleyan emphasis on personal initiative, itself inseparable from Wesley's own character, weakened the churchmanship, led in the coming years to secession and schism within the movement itself and so deprived it of the strength which Wesley had himself given it. A modern writer suggests that "its inability to translate this habitual mood (of Christian action) into anything more than personal and ameliorative activity" has been Methodism's greatest defect. If this is so, it is a defect that was ingrained in Wesley's own character.

But all saints have their weaknesses, St. Francis of Assisi no less than Ignatius Loyola or John Wesley. At Shoreham, Wesley once read a life of St. Catherine of Genoa which he found very indifferent: "I am sure this was a 'fool of a saint'." And he added: "Indeed, we seldom find a saint of God's making sainted by the Bishop of Rome," little knowing that he himself was among the number of those who have been canonized by Christian character. His faith was simple but fundamental. It was founded on the universality of sin; "wherever I have been", he wrote in 1773, "I have found the bulk of mankind, Christian as well as Heathen, deplorably ignorant, vicious and miserable". How was man's "diseased will" to be cured? Quite clearly, the grace of God was the only real effective agent just as it was also that which brought man to a realization of his possible salvation. "I believe no good work", he said, "can be previous to justification, nor consequently a condition of it; but that we are justified (being till that hour ungodly, and therefore incapable of doing any good work) by faith alone, faith without works, faith though producing all, yet including no good work." But Wesley was no Calvinist; it was Whitefield's Calvinism that led to the breach with John and his brother in 1740. There always remained a section of his own following which followed Calvin over election and predestination but this was not Wesley's own view. If man received faith, or rather if God bestowed faith upon him, it was open to him to achieve progressive moral perfection, "the restoration of the soul to its primitive health". In this scheme of things his redemption through the blood of Christ was the leading essential since it was this which enabled man to overcome the power of sin and gave him the faith and grace that would lead to good works and the throne of God.

It follows that Wesley emphasized above all the doctrine of moral and social responsibility. "I find more profit in sermons on either good tempers, or good works, than in what are vulgarly called 'Gospel sermons'," or again, "Christianity is essentially a social religion; and . . . to turn it into a solitary religion is indeed to destroy it." These sayings of Wesley may strike us as curious inasmuch as the texts of his own sermons were primarily doctrinal in the sense that they were concerned with faith rather than conduct. But this is not really a dilemma. Faith was the foundation on which good conduct rested. Wesley was, above all, concerned with the conversion of the soul to right action. The *Journal* contains innumerable illustrations of the bad man or woman who was moved to tears and repentance, found salvation and so trod the narrow way.

The pronounced emphasis on conduct had important social effects. Industry, gravity, thrift, contentment were compared with idleness, waste, dissipation, flippancy and discontent. Wesleyanism became a force of the greatest influence in fostering industrial development. It may be true that it tended to make the worker unduly content with his lot, but Wesley made it perfectly clear that he had the highest opinion of the worker who expected that he should receive fair treatment and fair wages at the hands of his employer. "The supreme economic virtue of industriousness was", as Dr. Warner puts it, "being bred into the fibre of Methodist character and endowed with a moral tone by an intense emotional experience." He quotes a contemporary verse which at once defines the scope of the argument:

> "*Where weavers expound as they sit at the loom,*
> *Where mechanics, inspired, the Gospel explain,*
> *And weave at a text as well as a chain.*"

The Wesleyan made a good workman, a responsible foreman, aware indeed of his own independence and his rights but not unduly antagonistic towards his employer. "To you", as the chemist Priestley put it, "is the civilization, the industry and sobriety of great numbers of the labouring part of the community owing."

The tendency of Methodism to instil loyalty and contentment among the working classes and to disavow attacks on contemporary authority was one of the reasons which led the great historian, Élie Halévy, to say that Wesleyanism was one of the forces which saved England from the French Revolution. This is indeed a correct adjudgement of the contemporary situation. The workman and his wife became interested in the politics of heaven rather than those of earth, and canalized his economic and political discontent in religious appreciation. Yet there was also another side to this. The Anglican Church had been woefully deficient in dealing with the working classes, had indeed very largely lost all influence over them in the growing industrial towns. When Wesley first came across the Kingswood miners, he found them totally ignorant of all religion, wild and dissipated. He gave some of them a new glimpse of reality which they had never before had the opportunity to investigate. What he did at Kingswood was copied all over the kingdom by other preachers, lay and clerical. They provided working-class men and women with a new interest, as well as the example of an honest, moral, clean-living life.

The religious side of nonconformity in showing the working classes of the late eighteenth- and early nineteenth-century England what Christianity might be, was a force of incomparable importance in England's social and religious development. It is no thanks to Anglicanism—with a few exceptions—that the English Socialist movement, unlike the continental movements, has always been closely attached to Christian ethics.

The Christian's individual responsibility was strongly emphasized by Wesley and so made the Wesleyan movement as a whole take a much more important part in humanitarian movements in the century than its numbers would have suggested. The eighteenth century, if not a particularly spiritually-minded age, was extraordinarily interested in humanitarian causes, in prison reform, in education, in improving conditions in workhouses and factories, and in abolishing the slave trade. John Wesley's creed had no time for the rich man who did not spend his riches for the good of others: "For upwards of eighty-six years", he wrote, "I have kept my accounts exactly. I will not attempt it any longer, being satisfied with the continual conviction that I save all I can, and give all I can, that is, all I have." His followers played a pre-eminent part in humanitarian and missionary movements which gave grace to social life in the last half of the century.

The span of Wesley's life very nearly covered that of the period itself. As a young man he had found the Church apathetic, wanting in divine energy, often slothful and worldly, above all lacking in divine enthusiasm. He had suddenly found the answer to the crisis of his time in the acceptance of a faith which seared life and gave it meaning and infinity. Perhaps he lacked patience, perhaps his missionary impulse was too un-intellectual, too dependent on what we may call the whole psychology of religious

F

revival. Certainly the attitude of the Anglican Church as a whole was unsympathetic and misunderstanding. Equally certainly he took upon himself functions which Anglican tradition had disclaimed. The administration of the rite of ordination, the structure and machinery of the Methodist Connexion, were departures from the past which could only be justified, if at all, by the contemporary situation. It was the greatest misfortune that the Church of England, less wise than the Catholic Church had been in the Middle Ages in relation to St. Francis of Assisi, was unable to absorb Wesley into her supremely elastic machinery.

Nevertheless, Anglicanism as well as Dissent owes Wesley an unending debt, in all the English-speaking parts of the world. For it was Wesley who reinvigorated religious life, who initiated the Evangelical movement as well as the Wesleyan and laid the foundations of the revival which in the long run abolished the abuses and the apathy, so current in Hanoverian England. It would be no exaggeration to say that Wesley was the most influential and most significant figure in eighteenth-century England. And all because he had analysed a disease and sought a cure. His brother, Charles, provided the movement with the poetry of song, George Whitefield with a once-fashionable eloquence, but it was Wesley who throughout dominated the situation. As he lay dying, his mind must have gone back to his Epworth days, to his mother, to Christ Church and Lincoln College, to Georgia and then to that gateway of unspeakable significance, the reading in Aldersgate in 1738. And he knew that, with all his faults, he had never deviated from his single intelligible loyalty to God. Exhausted by his illness, his age and his labours, he could just raise his arm and repeat: "The best of all is, God is with us," and then he said: "We thank thee, O Lord, for these and all Thy mercies; bless the Church and King; and grant us truth and peace, through Jesus Christ our Lord, for ever and ever." And finally before the last "farewell": "The Lord is with us, the God of Jacob is our refuge." But his work outlived him, a splendid monument to the faith of a truly religious man.

BOOKS FOR FURTHER READING

The Journal of John Wesley (Everyman, 4 vols).

The Journal, ed. N. Curnock (1900-1916).

Wesley's Letters, ed. J. Telford, 1931.

W. H. Hutton, *John Wesley*, 1927.

J. S. Simon, *John Wesley*, 5 vols., 1927.

M. Edwards, *John Wesley and the Eighteenth Century*, 1933.

W. J. Townshend, H. B. Workman and G. Eayrs, *A New History of Methodists*, 2 vols., 1909.

G. E. Harrison, *Son to Susanna*, 1937.

VIII. William Temple

THERE IS a great gulf between the world of Wesley and the world of Temple, far wider than the ninety years which separate Wesley's death from the birth of the future Archbishop would lead one to suppose. In the intervening period, the industrial revolution had reached its climax in England, making Britain the wealthiest country in the world, and had permeated other European countries as well as the United States of America. It left behind it a train of social and economic ills, "for all that glitters is not gold", which probably had a greater influence over the development of history than any other single theme. The predominance of the capitalist society was paralleled by the rise of the new national state and the victory of liberalism in politics as well as in theology. The rise of the State, illustrated by what happened in 1860 in Italy, in 1871 in Germany and in other countries at intervals all along the line ever since, may be traced to the growth in racial consciousness which had been so largely lacking before the French Revolution. To the French Revolution may also be traced the rise of liberal thought which depended on the widely accepted belief that man was both capable of and actually advancing towards perfection. Liberalism in theology has been rightly condemned because of its shortsightedness, but it was founded on a view of the contemporary world which was very widely accepted by intelligent men. The collapse of liberalism was succeeded by the appearance of a form of reaction in politics as well as in theology. In this sense it left a vacuum behind it which has never been filled satisfactorily. One other salient feature should be mentioned, the tremendous advances that have been made in science which convinced many that it was by science and science alone that man could achieve salvation. All these things were perhaps implicit in the structure of society before Wesley died. The march of invention evoked by economic necessity had led to the building of factories and new machines, to the great growth of industrial towns and a vast expansion of trade and wealth. The French Revolution was two years old before Wesley died. German theologians had already begun to examine the Bible from an analytical angle. Finally, in Priestley and Lavoisier, Buffon and Lamarck, to mention but a few, there were scientists whose experiments anticipated later developments. Yet more than a century, in point of value, separates Wesley from Temple.

Religious faith had not been immune from this change. Under the ardent stimulus of Wesleyanism the Anglican Church had somewhat reluctantly put itself into working order, more particularly after the Oxford Movement began to reassert the validity of traditional ideas in Anglican theology. Yet there was, and long remained, an undeniable tension in Anglicanism which reflected the later crisis of the secular world. If there were some sincere men who felt that the structure of faith and order was unalterable, there were many others who believed that the Church should try to condition its message to the new order of society and, quite apart from this tension within the Church, anti-clericalism became much more active without it. If a number of Anglican priests became Roman Catholics, an equally surprising number of extremely able men surrendered their orders because they could no longer accept its beliefs. The views of men like T. H. Huxley, Herbert Spencer, Samuel Butler and John Tyndall, all influenced the new generation, making it look with considerable suspicion at current theology. Long before the actual ritual of churchgoing ceased to be fashionable, theology had become intellectually disrespectable in a great many thinking circles.

That there was a greater crisis implicit in the world structure was not reflected visibly in the course of events until William Temple became a man. It might be said that his surroundings were favourable to success. His father, Frederick Temple, had had a brilliant career as Principal of Kneller Hall, then as Headmaster of Rugby, Bishop of Exeter, Bishop of London, and finally from 1896, as Archbishop of Canterbury. He was a great headmaster, continuing the tradition which Arnold had initiated at Rugby and combining firmness with sympathy. As a Bishop he met with opposition because of his association with *Essays and Reviews,* but his theology was eclectic rather than liberal. He was already an ageing man when his son, William, was born at the Palace, Exeter, on October 15th, 1881, but William retained the most lively veneration and affection for his father who died three months after his twenty-first birthday. It was natural that he should have followed his elder brother to Rugby where he was a scholar under the rule, first, of Dr. Percival, whose life he wrote, and then under Dr. H. A. James. From Rugby he went to Balliol, Oxford, as an Exhibitioner. This was the beginning of a long and devoted attachment to the University which he always cherished. Balliol was now at the height of its reputation as the centre of a classical tradition and of progressive thought (ingrained by Jowett). Edward Caird, who had succeeded Jowett as Master of the college in 1893, was a philosopher of eminence whose ideas and character influenced the undergraduate. He was a man of original mind who delighted in supporting radical causes, an unusual procedure among Oxford heads in the early twentieth century. It was he who had opposed the grant of an honorary degree to Cecil Rhodes and championed the admission of women to the University. His close association with the education of working-class men was another cause which soon attracted Temple. The latter's university career was uniformly successful, being crowned with the presidency of the Oxford Union Society in 1904 and a first class in classical moderations and in "greats". Shortly after he had taken his degree he was elected to a fellowship and lectureship in philosophy at the Queen's College, Oxford, a post which he held for six years.

The imprint of these years remained with him all his life. The dialectic and the idealism that he had learned from Caird remained the foundation of his political and religious thinking, even if it underwent profound changes in the coming years. He was ordained to the diaconate in 1908, to the priesthood in 1909. This was unusually late for a man of Temple's religious faith, but it is a sign of his feeling that he would only accept orders when he felt that he was fully fit to receive them.[1] There was a deliberation about this policy which shows that there was no sudden change of faith, no deviation from a secular job. He had intended that the priesthood should come in God's good time, but he had felt that there was no immediate haste. Yet his faith was already rich and fervent, enthusiastic and thoughtful. Two events illustrate this. As a member of the Student Christian Movement he was invited to act as a steward at the International Missionary Conference at Edinburgh, an experience which may have served to re-affirm what was to be his continual interest in the missionary work of the Church. The other event was the publication in 1912 of his first important piece of literary work, two essays in *Foundations*, a book sub-titled

[1] Bishop Paget of·Oxford had earlier been unwilling to ordain him because he suspected his orthodoxy!

"a statement of Christian Belief in terms of modern thought". One remaining factor dating back to his Oxford days must be mentioned, his close association with the Workers' Educational Association, of which he was one of the first members and President from 1908 to 1924. This represented his deep interest in the problem of education and society which formed a facet of his life from this time onwards until his death.

In 1910 he left Oxford for Repton where he remained four years. He was young in years and always remained so in spirits, but he was mature in thought. His departure for Repton was in a sense symbolic, for it meant that he was turning his back on the academic life of Oxford. Not that he ceased to write or think; he both wrote and thought as other great men talk, smoothly, almost unconsciously, always profoundly. He moved into the practical world of education, the world of what was in 1910 the entrenched, public-school tradition, too narrow to contain his broad vision. Yet the Repton years were a happy period, followed by an appointment to a London rectory, that of St. James', Piccadilly. This was as symbolic as the move to the headmastership; once again the traces were cut with academic life in order to fulfil what Temple now conceived to be the predominating mission of his life, to revive the life of the Church. Each phase of his career had so far reflected his inability to remain within the narrow fields of the particular post which he had held. At Oxford he had moved in circles outside the Queen's High Table, expressing the greatest interest in Dr. Stansfeld's work at the Oxford and Bermondsey Mission in Abbey Street, and in the plans for widening the educational facilities of the existing system. In 1910 he visited Australia at the invitation of Dr. J. R. Mott to spread interest in the Student Movement, another cause with which he was closely associated. All this had shown that behind the profoundly simple and satisfying faith which provided him with a mission in life there lay a certain disquiet with the life which he was leading. Although his time at Repton was unquestionably happy, he felt that he might be drenched in the administrative detail of headmastering. It was now that he branched ahead with his work.

The date was of course critical, not only because the change to Piccadilly coincided with the start of the Great War but because the beginning of the Great War was the symbolic conclusion of a period of world-history. Political and religious movements which had been developing in Temple's childhood were rapidly coming to a quite unforeseeable head. It was symptomatic that there was no obvious or close relationship between the two crises, for life no longer had a unitary meaning. There had once been a time when religion and life had formed a single whole so that a secular crisis had religious ingredients. But in some subtle way life's activities had become divorced from each other. It was natural, if perturbing, that the Church of England should have been chiefly concerned with the question of inter-communion raised by the Kikuyu business at the time that, as Sir Edward Grey suitably described it, the "lamps are going out all over Europe". What was the real strength and weakness of Anglicanism in 1914? Its strength lay chiefly in the devotion of its parochial clergy, in the re-invigoration of life to which both Evangelicals and Anglo-Catholics had equally contributed, and the beginnings of a more essentially positive theology. But there were also sundry weaknesses, some of which still continue, the disorder and irregularity prevalent in some parishes and dioceses which defiance of Anglican tradition had caused, the consistent inability on the part of a great many churchmen—Gore and Scott

Holland and the followers of the Church-Socialist League formed a notable exception—to face up to great social or political problems, the isolation of Anglicanism from other streams of Christian development—and its lack of freedom.

Yet these problems seem comparatively trivial besides the virtual collapse of world-civilization which the history of the next thirty years witnessed. The actual occasions of the wars of 1914 and 1939 were both comparatively superficial and irrelevant, the murder of an Austrian arch-duke in a sunny Bosnian town and the invasion of Poland by Germany on yet another sunny day just over twenty-five years later. What these wars really represented was the collapse of an economic and a political order. The intense national rivalries which had preceded the outbreak of war had been closely associated with the search for markets and raw materials or more plainly with the pursuit of what is usually called wealth. There were many signs that the capitalistic structure on which current economy rested had passed into a transitional stage which would either see its complete transformation or actual abolition and replacement by a new form of economy. The economic crisis was linked with the political because the validity of the political order could only be assured by economic stability or preferably economic expansion. Even in England which had been most touched by the economic expansion of the nineteenth century and the consequent increase in wealth and investment, there were clear signs that the predominance of Toryism and Liberalism was to be challenged by the rise of a new party which was actually opposed to the economic order. It was no accident that Temple was for a short time in 1918 a member of the Westminster Branch of the Labour Party. But it is probable that English and continental socialists were far more aware of the economic disease than of the proper cure.

In some ways, Socialism was only partly conscious of the political change that economic disorder was precipitating and that the Great War served to stimulate. It will be recalled that at the end of the Great War Germany lost the Hohenzollerns, Russia the Romanoffs, Austria the Hapsburgs and Turkey the Ottoman Royal house. Now this represented far more than the mere cost of defeat; it was the death of autocratic conservatism which had been disguised in some cases by semi-constitutional experiments. And it was at best extremely doubtful whether constitutionalism by itself could survive the collapse of the discipline (long in decay) represented by the old royal houses or the economic stability on which it had once rested, more particularly when constitutional democracy was so very loosely attached to spiritual realities. The post-war period was thus completely negative, not, as some commentators have insisted—degenerate, but merely negative. America reverted to Hardingite "normalcy" and traditional capitalism that gave rise to the tremendous economic crash of 1929-30. In Europe every country, with the possible exception of some of the smaller nations, watched the situation with extreme uneasiness. The Russian experiment marked both the complete overthrow of political and economic order as well as the replacement of constitutionalism, reflected in the rapid changes in 1917, by Marxist dictatorship. The republics of Austria and Germany were unstable politically and economically. Italy dismissed her incompetent socialist administration to embrace the mystical racialism of the efficient but brutal Mussolini. France witnessed the constant rise and fall of governments with increasing trepidation. In Spain the perilous antiquity of Bourbon government did not long survive the rule of one of the more incompetent dictators of modern Europe. While the great powers made sporadic and singularly unsuccessful efforts to stamp out the flames of war in Spain, Manchuria and Abyssinia, Caesaro-papism flooded in again on the stream of political reaction and economic crisis in Turkey, Germany and Spain. There was, it is true, an acute ideological clash, but this was in fact far less important than the incapacity of statesmen to face and to resolve the effects of the dissolution of political and economic order. The world slumped slowly but inevitably—slumped is the ideal expression—into the whirlpool of another great war.

But in this crisis of Church and State, which superficially seems so astonishingly different in scope and character, one thing is clear and important—that only an order which is founded on the recognition of spiritual realities can provide a solution. The work of the Church must continue to be impotent and concerned with apparent trivialities until it forces itself to realize that its task is no less than the redemption of the world. Important as its own business is and as essential to its high calling and spiritual efficiency, it is a lesson of history that the Church which fails to pierce the prevailing secular world with its message must gradually lose its following, and its place in society. The conduct of worship is the primary duty of the Church, but worship which is not reflected in the life of contemporary society is moribund. Similarly a state which seeks to exclude spiritual realities and to found its policy on vague moral uplift will never resolve the economic and political problems of the new world. What the twentieth century demanded then and now was an interlocking of function, an inter-relation of the fundamentals of the faith with the action of the state, the reconciliation of life and worship, so that the artificial and death-giving divorce between religion and life should be brought to an end.

It may be said here and now that no man showed so great an awareness of the problem or was so fitted to deal with it as William Temple. It is essential to bear this in mind in the brief narration of the course which his career was to follow after 1914. In that year he went to the well-paid rectory of St. James', Piccadilly, spending a great deal of time in the production of a Christian weekly paper entitled *The Challenge*. In 1916 the archbishops, suddenly aware of the irreligious state of the nation, initiated the National Mission of Repentance and Hope to bring to people the message of the Gospel in an effort to implement a religious revival. It is doubtful whether this mission left a very deep impress behind it, but it did at least open the eyes of Temple, who was one of its secretaries and who was to prove a master of the university mission type of address, to the disabilities from which the Church was suffering. " Don't you think", Dick Sheppard asked Temple, "we ought to have a ginger group in the Church of England?" Out of this grew the Life and Liberty Movement which was designed to give the Anglican Church greater freedom of government, launched at a crowded meeting at the Queen's Hall under the chairmanship of Temple in July, 1917. His interest aroused, nothing could stem his enthusiasm. He resigned his London rectory, thus dropping a very big slice of income, to travel the country and so spread propaganda for the cause. All was at last crowned with success, thanks, partly, to Temple's enthusiasm and partly to Archbishop Davidson's states-manlike co-operation, for the Enabling Act of 1919 led to the creation of a Church Assembly, composed of bishops, clergy and laity. This Assembly has the power to deliberate and formulate measures on Church government which only require parliamentary sanction before they become law. Despite the somewhat disturbing combination of age and experience, largely unsupported by youthful enthusiasm, the Church Assembly has initiated and passed many useful and necessary laws. It became the medium through which the Church could change its antiquated machinery and institute essential reforms, so that, in Temple's words, it "may the better fulfil its duty to God and to the nation and its mission to the world".

The passing of the Enabling Act did not in any way end Temple's continued interest in the problem of Church reform, but it allowed him once more to broaden his interests and to turn his attention to the manifold problems of the post-war world. For the third time he was offered and now accepted a Canonry of Westminster Abbey. Two years' later he left the abbey for the smoke-laden diocese of Manchester in succession to the great evangelical, Dr. Knox. At Manchester, eight years later at York and still later at Canterbury, he proved an entirely admirable diocesan. Where another man might have assumed that his studies or his participation at important conferences would have been his first duty to the Church to the neglect of his diocese, Temple proved, as all observers were agreed, a true "father-in-God". He tried to take a Friday off every week, but he never lost touch with the diocese, and was consistently hospitable, more particularly at Bishopthorpe, continuously approachable and full of affection for all with whom he came into contact, both young and old. It was this genuine pleasure in the company of others, the candour of his affection, his willingness to see the good in men which sometimes made him a poor judge of character, which left its deepest impress upon the ordinary man. Leeds undergraduates might, as Canon Baker observes, greet him with "Where have you been all the day, Billy Boy?" or a S.C.M. Conference at Swanwick shout to him: "Heil Ebor" without causing the least loss of dignity or diminution of respect; his laugh, indeed, echoed to the high heavens. It is perhaps one of the most striking facts of the really great man that he is strikingly ordinary. In a world where men so often stand on their dignity, where prelates are sometimes proud and often reserved, where office glorifies but does not halo, William Temple remained essentially human, as human as Francis, as loving as Wesley, as thoughtful as Hooker.

Unfortunately depth of character and the power of prayer are not in themselves sufficient to meet the requirements of the modern world. They must find their embodiment in an active message and in actual activity. Pietro Morrone was a saint but as Pope Celestine V he was an abysmal failure. Happily, if England's Archbishop never consciously deserted his diocesan duties, he had a broader vision of his duties to the world than that of a mere diocesan. Faced by the double crisis in the Church and the world, he saw that the answer to the problem lay in the reconciliation of the Church to the world and of the world to the Church. There were those who criticized comments which he made on the economic situation; Neville Chamberlain replying to a persuasive demand which Temple made on March 5th, 1934, to restore the "cuts" in unemployment allowances before he tried to reduce income-tax, commented: "When people take a hand, whose influence, in consequence of their position, is likely to be widespread, then I think they ought to weigh their words carefully if they desire to rush into print." But this was precisely the Archbishop's own view. It was because he weighed his words, because he valued human justice as an aspect of the divinely appointed national order that he sought to influence the direction of human effort to all departments of life. He had indeed some answer to the pressing problems by which the contemporary world was and is faced. "If we are to enter into the Life to which the Lord Jesus invites us, the self in us must be eliminated as a factor in the determination of conduct; if possible, let it be so effaced by love that it is forgotten; if that may not be let it be offered. For if we are to *come to the Father*, self must be either offered or forgotten."

The future biographer will come indelibly to the conclusion that the Archbishop's strength was spiritual first and foremost. This is again a *sine qua non* of religious greatness; that the *City of God*, the *Summa Theologica*, the *Institutes of the Christian Religion*, the *Spiritual Exercises*, the *Laws of Ecclesiastical Polity*, intellectually compelling as they may be, rest fundamentally on a faith that was profoundly rich. Temple owed much to his family, something to Streeter of Queen's, but more to his own care for the things of the spirit. Dr. Matthews has suggested that Temple had essentially the "believing" mind, that he was not encumbered by the doubts which have perplexed so many of his generation. Almost intuitively—and he himself held that his thought-process was itself intuitive and unconscious, he knew that he believed in the great spiritual realities of life. "What worship means," he writes, "is the submission of the whole being to the object of worship. It is the opening of the heart to receive the love of God; it is the subjection of conscience to be directed by Him; it is the declaration of the need to be fulfilled by Him; and as the result of all these together, it is the surrender of will to be used by Him." Worship was expressed for him in prayer—prayer that was instinctive with personal relationship, for "Not as mere appreciative intelligence do we pray, but as children who want to be with their Father, as friends who must mark off certain times to enjoy the company of their Friend," and in the acceptance of the Eucharist. "It is the family meal, where the children gather round the Table to receive what their Father gives them. And what He gives, through His incarnate Son, is His own nature; in other words, it is love.'' He used, perhaps above all, to enjoy the Celebrations in the country church of Bishopthorpe. Only a man with intense spiritual strength could face the immense responsibility of his position with equanimity and assurance.

Yet his faith had intellectual foundations. If the *Readings in St. John's Gospel* formed in some ways Temple's most significant contribution to religious literature, more particularly as they were written by the head of a great institution, his *Mens Creatrix, Christus Veritas* and more particularly his Gifford lectures, *Nature, Man and God*, reveal his profound intelligence and his significance as a religious philosopher. He had been an idealist in his early days at Oxford, but his deep conviction about the nature of objective reality made him into a realist. He owed far too much to Hegel and the dialectical school of philosophers to be a Thomist, though he had the greatest appreciation for Aquinas, and yet at the same time he felt that Cartesianism was by its nature one of the most damaging philosophies ever put forward. He started from the belief that the world was real, that mind was real, and that such reality must pre-suppose a Creator. If we doubt the validity of man's own judgments we shall find ourselves back in a world of subjective irrationalism which must deprive life of meaning. On the contrary, the world must be accepted as a reality and what occurs in human history therefore takes place in a genuine framework. Furthermore, man's own experience and own mental judgments presuppose that there is a rational quality in the governance of the world. If God is wholly transcendent to the world, He is equally wholly immanent within it. Revelation is not confined to a particular moment or moments in past history. It is a continual process, binding together the natural and supernatural order. It is impossible to do justice to Temple's thought in so summary a fashion, but it is important to remember that it was this combination of spiritual richness and mental balance which gave his judgment so much force and made his activities so vitally relevant to the world.

What may one say about his judgment and his activities? As a diocesan he did what he could to forward the life of the three dioceses over which he was called to preside, with what success those who have experienced his insight and sympathy may adjudge for themselves. As an Arch-bishop—he succeeded Cosmo Gordon Lang at York in 1928—he sought to bring the Church back into the life of the nation. "No department of human life", he said in a journal entitled the *Pilgrim*, which he edited from 1920 to 1927, "lies outside the scope of moral principle, and in none are the order of life and the maxims governing public action without influence on character. There is a frontier of the Church's legitimate concern, but it is not one that excludes any human interest; it only defines the Church's method of dealing with that interest." Thus although he was deeply concerned with the breakdown of family life which the gradually mounting figures of divorce, and later of venereal disease, revealed, he was equally concerned with the necessity for justice in economic life. He was largely responsible for the Christian Conference on Politics, Economics and Citizenship which met at Birmingham in 1924. Two years later he was one of the bishops who tried to mediate in the General Strike. In 1941 he took a leading part in the Malvern Conference called to "consider from the Anglican point of view what are the fundamental facts which are directly relevant to the ordering of the new society, and how Christian thought can be shaped to play a leading part in the reconstruction.'' There were many who misconstrued and misinterpreted his attitude, forming a relatively influential group which would have blocked, if they could, his appointment to Canterbury in 1942. His later views, which are admirably summed up in the Penguin Special, *Christianity and the Social Order*, represented his conviction that the only ordering of society which could bring justice and happiness to all men and women was that which was lived under the shadow of the natural law of God. ''A fundamental duty which man owes to God is reverence for the world as God has made it.'' It is for man to look God-ward and so promote the society for which God has created him.

He found another outlet for the integration of life and religion in ''the body of Christ'' in the part which he played in missionary conferences and in the ''oecumenical'' movement. ''As though in preparation for such a time as this,'' he told the people at his enthronement at Canterbury in 1942, ''God has been building up a Christian Fellowship which has extended into almost every nation, and binds citizens of them all together in true unity and mutual love. No human agency has planned this. It is the result of the great missionary enterprise of the last hundred and fifty years. Here is the one great ground of hope for the coming ·days, this world-wide Christian fellowship, the oecumenical movement.'' He played a prominent part at the Lausanne Conference on Faith and Order in 1927, and the International Missionary Conference at Jerusalem in 1928. He was always profoundly aware of the harm done through disunity to the robe of Christ, and he insisted that all Christian bodies were bound together as an ''organism of His Spirit'' to work for the ''redemption of the world''. He was sufficiently realistic to realize the great difficulties which prevented re-union nor was he willing to sacrifice principle for expediency. Yet he held that the acceptance of the Christian faith formed an underlying bond. It was his leadership and enthusiasm which made the second Conference on Faith and Order, held at Edinburgh in 1937, so notable a success. Whether by the green of Malvern Hills, grey stones of St. Giles, blue of Lausanne or white of Jerusalem, he knew that the unity of the faith formed a fundamental answer to the disintegrating world. "I believe", he told his listeners over the wireless in 1930, "that life and the world constitute a single whole. . . . I am convinced that nothing is now so important—for, indeed, the alternative is in the long run the collapse of civilization—as to reconstruct our whole fabric of thought and practice around the self-expression of ultimate reality in Jesus Christ as its focus and pivot and dynamic source of power."

"Nothing is now so important." He had already played a notable part in the reform of the Church's antiquated administration and if he had lived he would have done more. But there were signs that he felt increasingly that the only way to meet the crisis, which like a great thundercloud rolled forward over the world, was by a re-orientation of civilization around the Cross. He was never a pacifist, even if he liked and sympathized with the views of many of the group that used to meet at Canon Raven's house at Cambridge, but he saw that force by itself was powerless to stem the all-pervading malaise. His preaching took on a new urgency. In 1940 he went to Holland to meet continental Church leaders in an effort to find a solution which might shorten the war—in vain. He was the leading personality among the British clergy who insisted that the victors' peace aims must be consistent with their original pretensions. The power of evil could be only satisfactorily and finally overcome by the greater power of love which must remain no mere sentiment but a force pervading the whole social and international order.

In 1942 Dr. Lang laid down the high office which he had held with conspicuous, if at times much criticized, statesmanship. On St. George's Day Temple was enthroned as his successor in Canterbury Cathedral. He was relatively a young man—sixty-one. It was true that he suffered from gout and that his bulk had enabled the witty Ronald Knox to satirize him as long ago as 1912:

> "First, from the Public Schools—Lernaean Bog—
> No paltry Bulwark, stood the Form of Og,
> A man so broad, to some he seem'd to be
> Not one, but all Mankind in effigy."

But given ordinary circumstances, there seemed no reason why his archepiscopate should not have been as equally long as that of his predecessor. He was abstemious—sadly he reduced the sweets which he loved as he realized that they were bad for his gout—and careful, but the strain was tremendous. Within a few months of his enthronement, bombs rained down on the Close and set much of the cathedral city on fire. There was much to demand his attention; the new Education Act of 1944, rallies and conferences at great cities throughout the kingdom; the missionary work of the Church; the tremendous issues involved in the war—and the post-war settlement, as well as his business as a diocesan. He was always approachable, completely master of every subject, totally sympathetic. But on October 26th, 1944, while he was apparently recovering from gout at Westgate, he turned to his wife— Frances Anson whom he had married in 1916—and with the words "I feel very faint" collapsed and shortly after died.

Five days later, on All Saints Eve, a day marked by a continuous downpour of rain, the greyness of the cathedral was suddenly splashed with colour as the procession wound itself through the great doors to the cloister garth. The memories of Exeter and Rugby, of London, Oxford and Manchester, of jewel-like Grasmere and the heathered Quantocks on which he had loved to walk, of Bishopthorpe and the Old Palace passed in rapid succession and were dwarfed in the tremendous knowledge that momentarily at least the Church of God had lost the one man who saw clearly what the essential needs of the world (that had lost sight of spiritual realities or of an integrating factor that would make them real in life) were, and then fluted sound pierced the cathedral in the lovely and fitting words of the Welshman, Henry Vaughan:

> "*My soul, there is a country*
> *Far beyond the stars,*
> *Where stands a winged sentry,*
> *All skilful in the wars.*
>
> *There above noise, and danger,*
> *Sweet Peace sits crown'd with smiles,*
> *And One born in a manger*
> *Commands the beauteous files.*
>
> . . .
>
> *If thou canst get but thither,*
> *There grows the flower of peace,*
> *The Rose that cannot wither,*
> *Thy fortress and thy ease.*
>
> *Leave then thy foolish ranges,*
> *For none can thee secure*
> *But one, who never changes,*
> *Thy God, thy life, thy cure.*

And we passed out into the rain, content to remember that St. Augustine had written so long ago: "Thou hast made us for Thyself and our hearts are restless until they find rest in Thee."

Books for Further Reading

William Temple, *Mens Creatrix*, 1923.
     Christus Veritas, 1924.
     Christianity and the Social Order, 1942.
     Readings in St. John's Gospel, 1939, 1940.
     Nature, Man and God, 1932-4.

A. E. Baker, *William Temple and His Message*, 1946 (with a Memoir by the Bishop of Chichester).

A. E. Baker, W. G. Peck, W. R. Matthews, S. C. Carpenter, Carl Heath, F. Harrison, *William Temple, an Estimate and Appreciation*, 1946.

This book was completed before the publication of Dr. F. A. Iremonger's authoritative *William Temple* (1948).

Since this book was originally written a number of useful works have been published, which contribute to our understanding of the personalities under consideration.

St. Augustine

E. Gilson, *The Christian Philosophy of St. Augustine*, trans. Lynch 1961.

F. van der Meer, *Augustine the Bishop*, trans. Battershaw and Lamb 1961.

G. Bonner, *St. Augustine of Hippo*, 1964.

P. Brown, *Augustine of Hippo*, 1967.

R. A. Markus, *Saeculum, History and Philosophy in the Theology of St. Augustine*, 1970.

St. Francis of Assisi

O. Karrer, *St. Francis of Assisi*, trans. N. Wydenbruck, 1947.

R. B. Brooke, *Early Franciscan Government*, 1959.

M. D. Lambert, *Franciscan Poverty*, 1961.

O. Engelbert, *St. Francis of Assisi*; trans. E. M. Cooper, 2nd edition, 1965.

T. S. R. Boase, *St. Francis of Assisi*, 1968.

J. R. H. Moorman, *The Franciscan Order to 1517*, 1968.

St. Thomas Aquinas

F. C. Copleston, *Aquinas*, 1956.

J. Pieper, *Introduction to Thomas Aquinas*, 1963.

John Calvin

J. D. Benoit, *Jean Calvin*, 1948.

J. T. McNeill, *History and Character of Calvinism*, 1954.

R. M. Kingdon, *Geneva and the Coming of the Wars of Religion in France, 1555-63*, 1956.

W. Niesel, *The Theology of Calvin*, 1956.

J. Cadier, *Calvin*, 1958.

F. Wendel, *Calvin, trans. P. Mairet*, 1963.

St. Ignatius Loyola

J. Brodrick, *Ignatius Loyola*, 1956.

C. Hollis, *History of the Jesuits*, 1968.

M. Foss, *The Founding of the Jesuit Order 1540*, 1969.

Richard Hooker

F. J. Shirley, *Richard Hooker and Contemporary Political Ideas*, 1949.

P. Munz, *The Place of Hooker in the History of Thought*, 1952.

J. S. Marshall, *Hooker and the Anglican Tradition*, 1963.

John Wesley

U. Lee, *John Wesley*, 1958.

V. H. H. Green, *The Young Mr. Wesley*, 1961.

M. Schmidt, *John Wesley*, Vol. I (1703-38), trans. N. Goldhawk, 1962.

V. H. H. Green, *John Wesley*, 1964.

William Temple

O. C. Thomas, *William Temple's Philosophy of Religion*, 1961.

J. D. Carmichael and H. S. Goodwin, *William Temple's Political Legacy*, 1963.

Index